TAK...
LAND
PART ONE

RICK JOYNER

MorningStar Publications
A DIVISION OF MORNINGSTAR FELLOWSHIP CHURCH
375 Star Light Drive, Fort Mill, SC 29715
www.MorningStarMinistries.org

Taking the Land, Part One
by Rick Joyner
Copyright © 2008

Distributed by MorningStar Publications, Inc.,
a division of MorningStar Fellowship Church,
375 Star Light Drive, Fort Mill, SC 29715
www.MorningStarMinistries.org
1-800-542-0278

International Standard Book Number—1-59933-826-2;
978-1-59933-826-2

Cover Design: Kevin Lepp
Book Layout: Dana Zondory

Unless otherwise indicated, all Scripture quotations are taken from the New American Standard Bible, copyright © 1960, 1962, 1963, 1968, 1971, 1973, 1974, 1977 by The Lockman Foundation. Italics in Scripture are for emphasis only.

No part of this book may be reproduced or transmitted in any form or by any means, electronic, mechanical, including photocopying, recording, or by any information storage and retrieval system, without written permission from the author.

All rights reserved.
Printed in the United States of America.

Table of Contents

UNDERSTANDING THE VISION

This book is a prophetic look at what is already beginning to unfold. After wandering in the wilderness for an age, the church is preparing to cross her Jordan River and begin possessing her inheritance. This book is a look at the biblical blueprint that reveals what we can now expect to unfold.

Of course, many individuals have faithfully navigated the many wildernesses that are always found between the place where the promises of God are received and the Promised Land, or the fulfillment of those promises. However, what we are about to see is the corporate body of Christ finish her course. This holds unprecedented ramifications for both the church and the world.

The Lord has had His people praying for the coming of His kingdom for nearly two thousand years, and we can now see the day of the Lord beginning to dawn. His kingdom is at hand, and the foundation for it is already being laid. It is now time to prepare the way for the Lord.

The kingdom of God is coming. That is certain. For those who see, it is becoming more real and more clear. With the increase of all the troubles in the world, many would wonder how anyone could say that the day of the Lord is beginning to dawn, but there is another reality. We must have our spiritual eyes opened to see what others may not be able to see. Just as Moses endured as **"seeing Him who is unseen (see Hebrews 11:27)**, but saw a reality greater than what others could see, the reality of the coming kingdom is more real than anything else in this physical world. It will soon overcome all of the troubles in this world just as the sun overcomes the darkness when it rises.

The clouds of confusion and fear will soon yield to the Son who is already rising in the hearts of His people. This is where the day will first dawn—in the hearts of His people. Those who begin to see will walk in increasing light, peace, and joy as the world sinks into increasing darkness, fear, and confusion. This is because they will see and live in another reality. There will be an increasing contrast in the times ahead between the people who follow the Lord and those who do not. This will help many who have been living in darkness to see the light more clearly, and they will increasingly come to the light.

The Two Great Tasks

To prepare for the coming kingdom, there are now two great tasks for the body of Christ. One is for her to prepare as a bride for her coming Bridegroom. For this reason, many will be raised up with a special love and devotion for the church to become all that she is called to be. This is the zeal of the true friends of the Bridegroom—to help her to become the bride that He is worthy to have.

The second great task is for the church to help prepare the world for the coming of the kingdom. In Isaiah 40:3-5, we are told of the preparation that must be made for the coming of the King and His kingdom:

> **The voice of one crying in the wilderness: "Prepare the way of the Lord; make straight in the desert, a highway for our God.**
>
> **"Every valley shall be exalted and every mountain and hill brought low; the crooked places shall be made straight and the rough places smooth;**
>
> **"The glory of the Lord shall be revealed, and all flesh shall see** *it* **together; for the mouth of the Lord has spoken"** (NKJV).

The wilderness is a place where many other people will not be found, but that is the place where the voice will begin to be heard to prepare the way for the Lord. The great purposes of God rarely start with many but rather with the few. One person who sees and walks in the truth is more powerful than an army who will compromise the truth. Some are being raised up today who will never compromise the truth for any reason because they have been given the grace to see it, even to save their own lives. These are walking martyrs who die daily for the sake of the gospel—the gospel of the kingdom that will soon be preached throughout the earth.

How we prepare the way for the Lord is to make a highway. We travel highways every day, but we probably never think about those who with great effort built them, cutting through the mountains, swamps, dry places, thick forests, and underbrush so that we could have a level place to drive upon with ease. Such a highway for the kingdom has been under construction for a long time. We can now move ahead spiritually with ease over ground previous generations labored greatly to provide a way through. The job of every generation is to extend this highway for the next one. When it is complete, the kingdom will come and the glory of the Lord will be revealed so that all can see Him.

As Isaiah prophesied, this highway must be straight and level. Many things that are now exalted will be brought down, and many who are low will be brought higher. What are we now giving ourselves to—the things that will be coming down or the things that will be rising up? It takes eyes to see where to invest our labor in that which is low but destined to rise, just as it takes vision not to give ourselves to what may now be high but is destined to fall.

It is said that no successful person can make friends because once they are successful they cannot trust anyone's motives. To a degree this is true. Is that not why the Lord Himself came in such a lowly state, being born in a stable, raised in the most despised town in the most despised nation in the world? He purposely came in a way that the prideful and selfishly ambitious would not be attracted to Him. For this reason, Joseph of Arimathea was one of the most remarkable of all of Jesus' followers. He went and asked for the body of Jesus after His crucifixion. He made his commitment to Him when all seemed to be lost, and the Truth Himself was dead. Joseph obviously would rather take his stand with the truth, seemingly defeated, than a lie that is prevailing.

Throughout church history, at least a few in every generation had the resolve of Joseph of Arimathea, who would stand at any cost for the truth as they were given the grace to see it. They were the great witnesses who were the light of their times. We are now coming to the end of the age that is the harvest, the maturity of all that has been sown, and we will see many arise with the mantles of each of these great saints.

However, like any successful investment with people, we must be willing to "buy low and sell high." Those who are destined to be great in the kingdom may now be low. Those who make their commitment in someone when they are low can be trusted when the exaltation comes. That is why King David's mighty men, the administrators in his kingdom and his friends for life, were those who gathered to him when he was fleeing from Saul, living in caves, and looking like one with no hope for a future.

I was told nearly forty years ago that I would see the coming of the kingdom if I would keep "the heart of Simeon." Simeon was the old prophet who held the baby Jesus and could see in this mere infant the salvation of the world. Who today has such vision that they do not see people in their present condition but rather as they are called to be? These are already beginning to see the coming of the kingdom, and even though it may still be just the first rays of light, the dawning of the day is near.

What is our vision causing us to invest in? Are we investing in that which is about to be lifted up or that which is about to be brought low? My purpose in writing this book is to help open eyes to see what is to come, to see how we can help build this highway, and to help the bride make herself ready for the greatest of all human events—the coming of the King.

Throughout the church age, many have given themselves to these two great tasks, and much has been accomplished. There is also much left to be done by the last generation—maybe as much as all who have gone before them have accomplished. For this reason, there is a great speeding up of the preparation of those who have been called to this great task. All Christians who are living in these times have a part to play. We are here for such a time as this. No greater cause and no adventure is as exciting and fulfilling as what we have before us now.

A NEW PERSPECTIVE

In this book I will begin to present what may be a different view of the end of this age than you have heard before. I will not focus on the troubles at the end of the age, such as the great tribulation or the antichrist, but on what will be the greatest event at the end of the age—God's people walking in all of their benefits as citizens of the kingdom, and by this preparing the way for the kingdom to come.

The "good news" is not that this is the end of the age, but that it is the beginning of the one in which Christ will reign as King over the earth. He is not coming to condemn but to restore. He did not die on the cross so that He could condemn but so He could save, and that salvation includes both mankind and the whole earth. The Scriptures are clear that the earth will be restored to the paradise that it was originally created to be with "the last Adam," Christ, having recovered all that was lost by the first Adam.

The first step of this process of restoration must begin with the church, the bride of the last Adam, which will reign with Him in the age to come. The Scriptures are clear that the New Covenant is a better covenant, with more glory than the Old Covenant. We are entering the times when the glory of the New Covenant will be seen and demonstrated as truly a greater covenant. We will begin to see just how great the power of the cross is. The ultimate power of the cross is the resurrection, and we are about to see the resurrection power of the cross revealed against all forms of death, including all sickness, disease, oppression of the devil, and what has caused the release of this death—sin itself.

The Devil's Boast

The devil still has a boast that caused one-third of the angels to fall. His boast is that mankind, the special, unique creation of God, who He made to have a special relationship with, chose to rebel even while living in the perfect environment of paradise when given the choice between obeying God or following Satan. However, by the end of this age, the "last Adam," Jesus, will have a bride that even in the darkest of times will choose to obey Him. This will be a witness even to principalities and powers on every level that God's kingdom will certainly prevail, and the truth is stronger than any lie.

Every time we are in the midst of troubles, if instead of complaining we offer thanksgiving to God; instead of being depressed we rejoice; and instead of being fearful we trust Him, it is a testimony that the Word of God will ultimately prevail. In the most difficult times, the greatest worshipers are revealed. These are worthy to be trusted with the great authority that the Lord is about to give His people.

We are told in Psalm 100:4-5, **"Enter His gates with thanksgiving, and His courts with praise. Give thanks to Him; bless His name. For the Lord is good; His lovingkindness is everlasting, and His faithfulness to all generations."** The way to dwell in the presence of the Lord is to be a thankful person, which can open the door to Him every day, in every situation. We go deeper as we go further into praise. We do this because regardless of what the circumstances look like, He is good, He works everything for our good, and we can trust Him to fully prevail.

He has proven this faithfulness to every generation, and those who trusted Him became a light to their generation, showing the goodness and faithfulness of the Lord. Church history is the testimony that He has truly been faithful to every generation, and we are called to be a testimony of His faithfulness in our own.

While the systems of the world will be falling apart, those who serve His kingdom will be building. As we proceed into these times, there will be an increasing distinction between those who obey Him and those who do not. The reward of obedience and the repercussions of disobedience are becoming increasingly clear and are coming faster as we draw near to the end of this age, the beginning of the day of the Lord.

Moses was one of the great types of Christ in the Scriptures. The first time that he tried to be a deliverer for his people he was rejected by them. The second time he came in great power and set God's people free from their slavery. The Lord then made a distinction between His people and the Egyptians. He is about to do the same again because He is coming back for His people in unprecedented power.

As we begin to experience the increasing distinction between the people of God and those who are not His, this is going to be harder than we may think. To be building and prospering while others have their world collapsing, losing everything they have, will not be easy. It will be a cross to bear, but it must be done. All of man's idols, what he has put his trust in instead of God, will be destroyed. Only that which has been built on the rock of hearing the Lord's words and obeying them will stand. However, we are seeking to build on the rock not just for ourselves, but to be able to help pull others out of the quicksand. The Lord said that "the end of the age is the harvest" (see Matthew 13:39), because more will be coming to Him in these times than in all of man's previous history combined. When we build our lives on the rock, the stronger the construction, the more people will be able to save from what is to come. Every faithful life is a rock that will soon stand increasingly tall in this sinking world.

The Foundation of Understanding

To understand the end of this age, we must see it as a beginning more than an end. We will thank the

Lord for the end of this age like most of us are thankful every New Year when the old year is gone and there is the hope of a new one. Certainly the end of this age will be something to rejoice in, but it is not the end of the world, rather a new beginning for it. To understand what is now happening, we must begin to see it as a beginning, not the end.

Since 1855, Advent Movement eschatology (the study of the biblical prophecies of the end times) has become increasingly popular with Christians. This is because so many of the signs of the end of the age are now being fulfilled. However, most of the predictions of what would follow after these prophecies were fulfilled have almost never been accurate. Every honest seeker of truth must ask: "Where have the teachers who have been so devoted to this study been going wrong?" It is so obvious that most have.

First, there is the biblical and historic record that most biblical prophecies are not meant to be understood until after they have been fulfilled. Second, we have the biblical and historic record that those who have been the most confident to assert how biblical prophecy would be fulfilled have a record of accuracy approaching zero percent. All four of the Gospels make this clear. Those who most wanted and expected the coming Messiah not only missed Him when He came, but they were His greatest opposition and were the very ones who finally had Him crucified. This is a warning.

Those who were so devoted to the coming Messiah became His greatest enemies because He did not come in a form that they were expecting or wanting. It is a dangerous thing to be overly-confident in our own expectations, especially when they are colored with our own desires or prejudices. Every sect in Israel was confident that the Messiah would be one of their own, but He did not come as a part of anyone's camp. He was far above such a sectarian mentality and will be when He comes again.

We also have the testimony that even the Lord's disciples, whom He repeatedly explained things to in great detail, still did not really understand the prophecies until after they had been fulfilled—even the ones they were a part of making it happen! Even the greatest prophetic gifts "see in part" and **"see through a glass, darkly" (see I Corinthians 13:9-12 KJV)**. These gifts still have great merit and are necessary to prepare us for what is coming, but we must approach all prophecy with humility and openness to those who may have a part that we do not have.

Like Israel, we, the church, have a consistent record of rarely being able to predict just how biblical prophecies will be fulfilled. In the few cases in church history when I have come across a person or group that got one right, they only got part of it right, and the rest they missed. We might then ask: "What good is biblical prophecy?" It can still be a great help if used properly, like time markers which are able to give us general directions, but not for becoming dogmatic and presuming that we now know everything.

Even with the church's record of not being able to see the fulfillment of biblical prophecy accurately, many seem addicted to continuing to make this mistake. A noteworthy example of this folly was one of the best-selling books in the last few decades, *88 Reasons Why Jesus is Coming in 1988.* By 1989, it was clear that this was a miss, but it was amazing that so many actually bought the follow-up book, *89 Reasons Why Jesus is Coming in 1989.* I am not bringing this up to open old wounds, but we are called to understand the times. In fact, we should not be surprised by any major events that occur, much less the fulfillment of biblical prophecies. This is a noble endeavor, but we must also acknowledge that something has been seriously flawed in how we have approached this to date.

I certainly do not presume to have all of the answers either, but I obviously think I have some or I would not have written this book. I do not presume that I would have done better than any others if I had been limited to their resources at the time. Now we do have their record, which is grace from the Lord—if we use it right.

Acknowledging the failures of the past can be the beginning of a more accurate understanding if we learn from them. The record of the church demands humility, and the humble are the ones that God gives His grace to. Besides the many outright misses that so many teachers of biblical prophecy have made, there have been even worse tragedies that have taken place with some who were actually on target with some of their predictions. One of these was Andrew Murray, one of the great Christian voices in the nineteenth century, who accurately foresaw the coming of "another Pentecost." However, because it did not come in the form that he was expecting or through the ones he was expecting it to come through, he rejected it. Even though Murray did not receive the blessing he had desired and predicted, he still accomplished much in helping to prepare the way for it.

Moses also fell short of being able to enter the Promised Land, but he is unquestionably one of the greatest of all prophets, and he at least was able to get the people of God to the point where they could enter the land. The same happened to John the Baptist, who prepared the way for the Lord and even baptized Him but was obviously disconcerted by the form that Jesus' ministry took. Even so, Jesus never rejected John the Baptist, but commended him as the "greatest man ever born of woman" (see Matthew 11:11). However, He also made it clear that even the least in the kingdom of God would be greater than John.

A Better Covenant

What makes someone "great" in the eyes of the Lord may be very different than what makes them great in the eyes of men. John the Baptist did not perform any miracles, and those who will prepare the way for His second coming obviously will have great power, but there is much more to this. John lived in a time when the Spirit came upon men. His Spirit now lives in us. We do not build temples, we are temples. This is unquestionably greater.

18

That the Lord would say that the least in His kingdom would be greater than John is an amazing statement and should be a cause to rejoice, not out of pride but with even greater soberness. To whom much is given much is required, and we have a lot of work to do.

Even though John the Baptist was the greatest of the old order, the Old Covenant, we have a New Covenant that is truly "a better covenant." As stated, before the end of this age the glory of the New Covenant will greatly overshadow all of the glory of the Old Covenant. We are told in II Corinthians 3 and other places, that the glory of the New Covenant will actually be so great that it will make the Jewish people jealous. Before the end of this age, we can count on this being demonstrated and fulfilled. Therefore, one of our most important devotions must be to walk in the New Covenant—all of its benefits and all of its power.

We have certainly been blessed beyond measure to live under the New Covenant. Again, this is not a cause for pride or for comparing ourselves to others, but to whom much is given much will be required. It will be far worse to bury so great a treasure. How much more will this be to have lived in the greatest of times and not even discerned them? It is right that we devote ourselves to this understanding, and we should have a great appreciation for all who devote themselves to eschatology, but at the same time there is no science or formula that is going to enable us to understand prophecy correctly. However, God reveals mysteries. He is the One we must seek.

As we proceed, let us keep in mind that even if we are able to see some things clearly and accurately, we are still seeing in part and knowing in part. Again, to have the whole picture we must have the humility to be open to the parts that have been given to others. We will say more about this later, but the body of Christ will always be blind to the degree that she is lacking in unity. Even in the eschatologies that have proven to be wrong, these may have some parts with merit that should not be thrown out. Everyone who seeks will find, and everyone who has sought understanding from the Lord in any of these matters has found something. Many go on to add their own opinions to what they were shown and start missing because of this, but with all we will find some treasure we should not throw out.

As stated, I will be presenting a different eschatology than you have heard about before in this book, and yet in some ways it may seem very familiar. This is because I have kept some parts from every eschatology and have studied and included it where I think it fits. Even so, you have a right to ask what makes what I say any different from the others who have presented prophetic scenarios of these times. The real proof of a prophetic perspective is if it comes true or not.

One timetable set by a number of prophecy teachers was that the Lord would return within forty years of the Jewish conquest of Jerusalem in 1967. This is because it was said "that generation" would not pass away until all of these things were fulfilled (see Matthew 24:34). Many have concluded that a biblical generation is forty

20

years, but forty years passed in 2007 and the Lord did not return. Obviously there is a part missing to this prophecy.

Even though this forty-year prediction was obviously not accurate, we have the amazing prophecy of the Jewish people being gathered back to their land again, a second time, which is a clear biblical prophecy that has been fulfilled in our times. This is a clear sign that we are entering the very end of this age. Even so, we also need to question if even today Jerusalem is not still "trodden under foot" by the Gentiles because neither Jew nor Christian can even pray on one of the holiest of sites in Jerusalem, where the temple once stood.

Many other biblical prophecies about Jerusalem in particular seem to be coming to pass now. As some have pointed out, the Greek word translated "generation" in these texts actually means "a race." Their contention is that this was a prophecy, and even though there now has been a concerted effort to wipe out the Jewish people, this would never be accomplished—they will not pass away.

Even so, some very clear biblical timetables do indicate we are in a one hundred-year period in which we can expect this age to end and the day of the Lord to begin. This period is also corroborated by some of "the early church fathers," whose letters may not have been canonized but were considered to be authentic, making it quite clear that the first-century apostles and prophets thought the end of the age was going to be about two thousand years later. We will examine some of these in later studies.

For now, though there is a clear biblical prophecy about the timing of the end of the age, the timing itself is give or take one hundred years, an ambiguity that I think the Lord purposely left to give us a general time because that is all we need. It could be this year or it could be one hundred years from now. Even if it is one hundred years from now, we do not have any time to waste. Our main goal is not to get the times right, but to get right for the times.

BE CAREFUL HOW YOU LISTEN

"Therefore be careful how you listen…"
(Luke 8:18).

The above Scripture is an interesting and crucial exhortation. Of course, we should be careful about what we listen to but we must also take care about *how* we listen. Understanding comes from the words to "stand under." It implies trying to stand under another person's position in order to see and hear from their perspective. This is a rare gift. Many Christians drift from the understanding of the Scriptures because they begin to read them subjectively instead of trying to read them from God's perspective. They hear others and even the Lord in the same way, through their own perspective rather than His. Understanding requires that we go beyond this subjective and self-centered perception to see with His eyes, hear with His ears, and understand with His heart.

A dramatic example of not hearing right is the fact that every person who has come to me saying they had received a word that the Lord is coming soon was right, and He did come soon—for them! I'm serious—they died. To date, I do not remember a single example when this did not happen. One of the most dramatic was a young man of just nineteen who was a new believer. He recognized me and James Robison in a restaurant and came up to tell us how he had just received a word from the Lord that He was coming very soon. When he left the restaurant on his motorcycle, he did not even make it through the next stoplight.

Was that a tragedy? No. As we are told in Philippians 1:6, the Lord does not begin a good work in us that He does not intend to finish, and it was obvious that He had already finished the work He wanted to do in that young man. His word from the Lord was used to greatly comfort his family and friends. His time was up, and who knows what the Lord might have spared him from had he continued on in this life. The will of the Lord is far more precious than this life, and this young man's life and death were used by Him. That young man is also far happier right now than he ever could have been in this life.

I have also known quite a few people who were sure that they would not die but would be raptured. However, they were wrong because they died. So I really don't like to hear either of these statements from people, but let's go a bit deeper. We need to ask: "What difference does it make if we die or are raptured?" If we die, we are raptured! I think it is time we matured beyond this and just resolve that we are going to abide in the Lord, do His will, and accomplish His purpose for us in our generation. If we are in the last generation of this age that is fine, but if we are not, let's help prepare the way for the next one. Let's do all we can to go as far as we can and make the way smoother for those who follow.

We could say accurately that almost all biblical prophecy is presented without a specific timing. We are even told that the prophets who gave the prophecies did not know the timing or the manner in which their prophecies would come to pass. Most of the wrong predictions people have made when interpreting biblical prophecy were caused by trying to put a timeframe on it, and in almost every case this timing revolved around them. Even when the first apostles kept asking Jesus when things would happen, He replied that it was not their place to know, but basically that they had all of the information they needed to do their jobs.

Understanding Is Coming

Even though we may not have become mature enough to handle knowing the times, it is obvious in Scripture that as the end of the age draws near we will need more prophetic clarity—then we will begin to know the times of the Lord. This does not mean that we will ever know the time of His coming, but there are biblical indications that at the end we will begin to see His timing in things. We will cover this in a bit more depth later. For now, we must learn not to try and interpret everything so subjectively if we are going to understand the Scriptures or prophecy accurately.

The Lord told Daniel to seal up the prophecies that he was given and that they would be opened at the end of the age. We can expect this to begin happening with the Books of Daniel and Revelation. We are also told that "in the last days" the Lord would pour out His Spirit, and the consequences of that would be dreams, visions, and prophecy (see Acts 2 and Joel 2). This prophetic revelation coming upon His people is one of the great signs that we truly are entering the last days. However, this is not just for a sign, but because we are going to need the much more specific guidance of prophetic dreams, visions, and prophecy in these times.

To be trusted with more of this, we need to be found trustworthy, which means we will not keep adding our own opinions to what we are given. We must be content to get a part, keep it a part, and not try to make it the whole revelation.

Getting Personal

I now have over thirty-five years of operating in prophetic gifts. I have witnessed big mistakes in handling revelation and big successes. I have tried to learn from each one. I have been shown that a much greater prophetic ministry is going to be released than any are yet experiencing on the earth. Ultimately, there will be prophetic ministries that eclipse anything experienced under the Old Covenant.

I would like to walk in this, but I have tried to keep my goal in this life to hear on that great judgment day,

"Well done, good and faithful servant" (see Matthew 25:21 NIV). I know that being overly-concerned about what people think of me, either good or bad, will be a stumbling block to that ultimate goal. So I try to keep it simple, do the best that I can to obey the Lord, and receive my encouragement from Him. Even so, to date I think I have a pretty good record in the prophetic perspectives that I have shared. Please excuse me briefly as I defend myself a bit, which is a subjective perception, but I am doing this because of the instruction in this.

When I wrote *The Harvest* in 1988 almost everything in it seemed a stretch, even to me. Most of it has now come to pass. Many other prophecies that I have shared over the years have also come to pass. Over the years, I have also stood either alone or almost alone in many prophetic perspectives. I do not think it is profitable to go over each one, but just a couple, again for the instruction. I am also not claiming to be infallible because I do not believe anyone is. As soon as we start to think that we are infallible, we are in the most danger of falling.

I am still accused by some of making some wrong predictions that I did not make, but in fact was right about, such as Y2K. I was almost the only prophetic voice with a large platform at the time which said clearly that Y2K was not going to be anything. Even most of my close prophetic friends got caught up in the Y2K fervor. I think I am accused of this too because of my association with some of them. However, during the fervor of Y2K, it was hard to get anyone to listen or hear me.

As stated, there are other things that I have stood almost alone in saying which were contrary to the opinion of others and turned out to be right. I am not saying this to defend myself, though certainly there may be some of that in me. We must have a higher standard of judging prophecy to make it through the times ahead so that we can be trusted with more. We are going to need much more strategic prophecy to navigate safely and effectively through the times to come. We must rise to a new level of accountability and trustworthiness.

Even so, having your words constantly distorted, misunderstood, or misinterpreted comes with this territory in ministry. If they have done this to the Lord's own words and the Scriptures, we must expect the same. We must also come to a place where we just don't worry too much about those who distort or misunderstand our words, and go on seeking greater understanding and clarity for those who can handle them. As Peter wrote of Paul's teachings, the **"untaught and unstable" (see II Peter 3:16)** will distort them just as they even distort the Scriptures. Even so, there is a need for a higher standard of devotion to truth, accuracy, and integrity in these times of increasing confusion.

Seeking the Spirit of Truth

Those who have a **"love of the truth" (see II Thessalonians 2:10)** will not be deceived in the last

28

days. I have been convicted about how I have mishandled details as well. By loving the truth, we will be devoted to accuracy, even in the details. More than just having corrected our own words that are misunderstood or distorted, we need to understand what causes us to do this. These distortions are causing bad consequences now, but in the future it will be life or death for those who cannot discern the Spirit of Truth from the spirit of error.

As I am called to be a part of the eye of the body, I must take this personally. We do have a serious vision, hearing, and seeing problem in the church, and this is happening on my watch. Even when the prophecies are stated as clearly as they should be, they often get very distorted, even by those who love the prophetic. A couple of years ago, a friend of mine was asked if he had the timing on a coming disaster, which he had been shown would come to the West Coast. His reply was that it would not happen before October of that year. He said this because every year, on the Day of Atonement, which that year was coming in October, the Lord has shown him major events such as this that were coming, and he had not been shown any major events for that year. However, it was then widely reported that he said that it *would* happen after October that year, which he never said or even thought.

My friend, Bob Jones, whom I have never known to miss in a prediction received in a dream or vision, even when he gives dates and specific details, does at times share things in a way that could be easily misunderstood. Therefore, we need more clarity and accountability in the prophetic that would help to clear up some of these misunderstandings. I, too, have found that I should have been more clear in how I stated some things which were misunderstood.

An interesting fact that illustrates our need for discernment and a devotion to accuracy is the following: It has been estimated that the "fact" that Albert Einstein failed math in school, which has been published over one-half million times to date on the Internet, actually is not true. He was either at the top of his class or right at the top every year, and he never once failed math. The well-established and verified truth about this can be found on one website, which is in German. The point is that just because something is in print or published, especially on the Internet, or is even widely-believed, does not make it true. In fact, we should be more suspicious of what is posted on the Internet. It is a platform that allows anyone to say anything, and it can get picked up and widely-quoted, but still be wrong.

Confusion, distortion, and deception are increasing in the world. This is why the media has lost its credibility to the degree that journalists are now trusted even less than lawyers or preachers. There are journalists, lawyers, and preachers who live by the highest standards of integrity, but their reputations can be tarnished by just a few in their profession or calling who do not have the highest standards. Even so, in general, a terrible distortion and confusion of reality is taking place. We must resolve in our hearts that we are not going to compromise the truth, but we are going to seek the truth.

We must raise our standards of handling the word of God more carefully, especially those who are entrusted with prophetic revelation from Him and are totally devoted to truth and accuracy. If we would do this, we might be found trustworthy enough to be given far more. We are going to need far more accurate prophetic vision and revelation for the times to come. Our basic commodity is truth, and if we compromise this, everything that is built on it will be weak.

The Source of This Prophecy

The following prophetic scenario came mostly through dreams and visions, not my study of biblical prophecies. Almost all that I am sharing here I did later see in the Scriptures—most of the verses I will supply, and the perspective that I share will be based on them.

I have also gained some of my prophetic perspective from viewing historic events that I was shown by the Spirit to be prophetic parallels of what is to come. I will also supply some of these; however, I am unable to supply many of these because I simply have not kept up with them. One reason why I do not allow myself to be called a historian, but rather a student of history, is because I approached it in an unscientific, unsystematic, and subjective way. Much of what I now write and share I learned through research in which I was trying to find answers to my own personal questions and was not considering at the time that I would share it with others, much less ever write it. I do believe that all I share can be verified in the historic records, but

I do not have time to do this with all of the duties and responsibilities that I presently have. I hope to have the time in the future to do this. This is a flaw for which I am now apologizing. Even so, I have not written anything that I am not convinced is the truth and which I do believe a more skilled researcher will be able to corroborate. I also trust the Holy Spirit to lead everyone that really loves the truth enough to seek it.

As stated, I have studied a wide spectrum of eschatology, and I feel that almost all of them do have a valid "part" of the picture. After a time, I could see these parts fitting into a picture that was quite different from any others that I knew of—until I started reading "the early church fathers." These begin with the writings of the direct disciples of the Lord, and the first apostles, such as Irenaeus, a disciple of John, Polycarp, a disciple of Peter, and so on. Though those who served into the fourth century are often called "early church fathers," there is a great deal that can be learned from their writings. I was especially drawn to the earliest simply because in any research, original sources are important, and these are about as original as we can get. I feel that many of their writings corroborate the vision that I am sharing in this book.

By the way, the writings of the early church fathers absolutely establish the validity of the New Testament writings. Through their quotations of the letters of their mentors and others, the entire New Testament can be rebuilt with the exception of just eleven verses, none of which deal with important doctrines or prophecy. No other book has this kind of scientific validation with the exception of those parts of the Old Testament which were verified by the Dead Sea Scrolls. What has been handed down to us is the Word of the Lord, just as He gave it. Just as the first Fall came because the devil was able to tempt Eve into doubting what God had said, the beginning of every doctrinal fall will usually begin with the devil getting us to doubt God's Word, especially the Scriptures. There is an overwhelming mountain of evidence that the Scriptures are true, and if we are going to walk by the Spirit of truth, it is basic that we establish ourselves firmly on the written Word. If the One who was the Word, Jesus, would take His stand when tempted by the devil by declaring, **"it is written," (see Matthew 4:4-10)** how much more must we do this?

I have also found others throughout church history that shared my present perspective on the end times, even though they may have come to these conclusions in various ways. This was encouraging, and there is value to the teachings of our spiritual fathers and mothers we should honor, but the real test is always Scripture. That is always the ultimate original source, coming from or specifically anointed to be the basis of all doctrine by the Word Himself.

The Wrong Turn

I am not presenting this vision as the whole picture, but just the part that I have been given. I think it is accurate and true or I would not be presenting it, but

I also consider that it is incomplete without the other parts. A friend once told me what I believe to be a truth, "Almost all heresy is the result of men trying to carry to logical conclusions that which God has only revealed in part." This has been the root of some of the worst mistakes, errors, and heresies that have so often beset the church. We must learn not to try and explain or speculate about what we do not understand, but rather admit that we do not understand it. I have tried to do that here, which is why, at times, it may seem that I have stopped short of a conclusion. I have.

Other times I will share something as an opinion. The Apostle Paul did this, so I think it does give us liberty. However, we need to make it clear when it is an opinion rather than a revelation.

Another primary problem I feel can lead us astray is to give more attention to what the antichrist is going to do than what Christ is doing. Of course, we are not to be ignorant of the devil's schemes, and we need to heed the clear biblical warnings about the things that will surely come upon the world at the end, but they are not the main thing happening and should never have most of our attention.

The Right Path

We can have a complete and accurate understanding of the end of the age and still be deceived if we are not in God's will, doing what He has called us to do. Likewise, we may not have much understanding at all about these things but be perfectly in the will of God, doing what He called us to do. Given the choice, I would certainly take the latter. However, we do not have to choose between these, rather keep the main thing the main thing—which is following the Lord, obeying Him, and seeking to do His will in all things.

In this prophecy, you will read much more about what Christ is doing than about what the antichrist is going to do, has done, or is doing. If we as Christians begin to understand who we are in Christ and who He is in us, we will not fear any antichrist or any other person or spirit who serves the enemy, but rather they would fear us much more. Many tragic fears have gripped large numbers of Christians because of a wrong perception of these times, causing them to shrink back rather than to arise and become a part of the light which will prevail and is greater than any darkness.

More than just learning facts and details about what is to come to pass, let us always seek to know Jesus and follow Him more closely. All things came together through Him, and all things will ultimately be summed up in Him, so all things that are true will lead us closer to Him.

A New Breed of Ministry

A new order of leadership is about to arise in the body of Christ. Just as Joshua was different from Moses, this new leadership will be of a different nature than what the church has been accustomed to in her wilderness. Moses was more of a pastor, but Joshua was a military leader. We can expect this type of change to now emerge in the leadership of the church.

That there is a "new breed" of leadership is not a slam on the present leadership. Just as it could be argued that Moses was the greatest leader of all time, we are living in the times of some of the greatest missionaries, preachers, pastors, and leaders on all levels since the first century. Even so, there is a generation arising that is being prepared to walk in greater spiritual authority than anything yet experienced in the church age—with power, glory, and impact.

The coming generation will be resolute to advance and take spiritual territory that is their inheritance. They will also have the wisdom to know how to hold onto it. Their whole purpose will be to prepare the way for the kingdom of God to come to the earth, so that the Lord's will is done on earth just as it is in heaven. They will do this by their uncompromising devotion to do the will of the Lord and to submit to the authority of the kingdom. Because of their obedience, they will be entrusted with greater authority.

When the coming new breed of leadership begins to emerge they will inspire Christians everywhere to rise up, cast off all forms of rebellion and lukewarmness, and walk in the inheritance that was gained for them by the cross of Jesus. Christians will begin to walk in all of the benefits of their citizenship in heaven. In Acts 20:32 Paul spoke of **"the word of His grace, which is able to build you up and to give you the inheritance."** That is the word for this hour and the word that this book is devoted to. It is the **"word of His grace"** that will build up and fortify God's people and lead them to their inheritance in Christ. The grace of God is going to take on a whole new meaning and depth.

What I am sharing is already beginning to unfold. It is in the first stages and will unfold over years, but it has begun. These are the times of miracles and wonders. It is a wonderful change to no longer be hearing that "something is about to happen," but to instead hear "it is happening!" The coming generation will not be content to just read their Bibles and be encouraged by the great things God has done—they want to see the same great things in their own lives. That is true faith in God and in the Bible. His name is "I AM," not "I WAS" or "I WILL BE." He is the same today as He was in biblical times, and as the Bible declares, He has even saved His best wine for last. The coming generation will not settle for anything less.

Spiritual breakthroughs are now happening in many places. Others are witnessing a great mobilization of the army of God. We are entering the most exciting, difficult, and wonderful times the world has known. The kingdom of God truly is at hand, and a mighty army is being gathered to proclaim the gospel of the coming kingdom and to prepare the way for the King. However, Christianity in its present form will not be able to accomplish this great task. The church is going through a metamorphosis and when it emerges, the change will be as radical as that of a caterpillar which after being confined to the earth, becomes a butterfly that can soar high above the earth.

A Perpetual Youthfulness

One of the great miracles we will see is that this "new generation" which is rising up includes many who are in their 80s or even older. Just as Abraham, the "father of faith," was even older when he was called and then had to wait decades to see the promises fulfilled, sometimes the greatest faith of all is demonstrated when our physical bodies are fading. So our faith is not in our physical bodies or ourselves, but in the Lord to accomplish His purposes for us. This is not about physical age or spiritual age but about heart.

King David was a new generation man who saw the age of grace a thousand years before it came. He did not just see it and believe it was coming—he began to live in it a thousand years before the time. Today there are many who live nearly two thousand years after the age of grace had come and yet still live under the law. Again, being a new generation person is not about our physical age but about the age that we live in.

A true renewal is available for every believer, regardless of how far from this grace they have lived in the past—this is about grace! The entire first generation of Israelites to leave Egypt had to perish in the wilderness before the emerging one could cross over into their inheritance. This does not have to happen with the church, but the entire slave mentality that came with the people out of the wilderness must die. No one has to be left behind. It is the old nature that must die, and if we will let it, we can be renewed and go forth as a part of this new breed. Great grace is coming for renewal. Granted, change is a difficult thing for people, especially the religious who tend to put their confidence in a form, a style, and their own performance rather than God. Even so, grace is coming for even the most rigid if they will but take the leap of faith required.

As stated in Acts 20:32, **"the word of His grace"** builds us and leads us to our inheritance. Joshua and Caleb lived by this word. The result was that even though they saw all of the same conditions that the other ten spies saw—the giants, the walled cities, and other obstacles, they interpreted what they saw through God's grace or God's empowering and providing, instead of through their own weaknesses like the other spies did. The other spies thought that the giants would eat them, but Joshua and Caleb thought that the giants would be bread for them! They saw the same things, but they saw through the eyes of God's ability and power, not their lack of these.

The new generation can likewise see the same thing as everyone else but will interpret what they see differently. We are living in increasingly cynical times, so this is the best opportunity of all for true faith to be demonstrated. When everyone else is seeing through the eyes of fear and doubt, and their hearts start failing them for fear of the things coming upon the world, some will see and manifest the greatest glory and the greatest victories of faith. These live by **"the word of His grace" (see Acts 20:32)**.

The Devil's Basic Scheme

On September 11, 2001, a handful of terrorists had an almost unprecedented impact on the world. They caused stock markets around the world to plummet, erasing hundreds of billions of dollars in assets overnight, and for a time, caused almost the whole world to wonder if the systems of the world were collapsing. For many days, I was constantly contacted by major newspapers and other media who wanted to know if these things had been seen prophetically and what did they mean. Our website went from receiving a few thousand hits a day to over a million. For a couple of weeks, churches around the world broke attendance records. People were desperate for answers—to know what these things meant.

It is still hard to measure the monetary cost of 9/11, but even greater than that was the psychological impact it had. The fear barometer in America probably rose higher and more dramatically than it had even after the attack on Pearl Harbor. The attack on September 11 was so irrational, outrageous, and inexplicable that it is probable that never before in history had so few people had so much impact on the mentality of the whole world in such a short period of time.

All flights were grounded and multitudes of people were stranded all over the nation and the world. If they were trying to come into America, many did not know how or when they would get home again, exacerbating the impact of this attack even more for so many who were separated from loved ones. After September 11, much of the fear turned to anger, but overall the fear barometer stayed at a level considerably higher than before.

This is important for us to understand because the devil controls and brings people into bondage through fear, just as the Lord sets people free with His truth that imparts faith. Fear binds but faith sets free. The devil got a bigger grip on the world on 9/11, and though his grip may have been loosened slightly since then, we can be sure he is planning everything he can to get a stronger grip in the future, and it will come through fear.

The effect of increasing fear at the things coming upon the world has greatly increased the incidence of panic attacks, depression, even things such as hesitancy in relationships, both international and personal. Many businesses might never admit it, but they are determined not to hire Muslims. Some communities do not want them in their neighborhoods, and some businesses and communities do not want those of any religious persuasion.

Coming Faith Attacks

However, just as the enemy came in like a flood in this way, the Lord will raise up a standard against him. The Lord is also going to display His power in a way that likewise gets the whole world's attention. The Lord obviously does things much differently than the devil, but He is going to counter the fear with faith. Great spiritual exploits will cause awe and wonder across the earth. In place of panic attacks, His people are going to start having "faith attacks," with His faith coming upon them suddenly to do these great exploits.

Instead of being terrorists who spread fear and death, God's messengers will spread hope, faith, and life. Gospel bombs will start hitting every community until there will be nowhere on earth that one can escape the witness of the good news of the coming kingdom and the accompanying demonstration of its power. The darker it becomes in this world, the more His glory is going to be revealed, just as we read in Isaiah 60:1-5:

"Arise, shine; for your light has come, and the glory of the Lord has risen upon you.

"For behold, darkness will cover the earth, and deep darkness the peoples; but the Lord will rise upon you, and His glory will appear upon you.

"And nations will come to your light, and kings to the brightness of your rising.

"Lift up your eyes round about, and see; they all gather together, they come to you. Your sons will come from afar, and your daughters will be carried in the arms.

"Then you will see and be radiant, and your heart will thrill and rejoice; because the abundance of the sea will be turned to you, the wealth of the nations will come to you."

We see here that at the very time darkness is covering the earth and deep darkness the peoples, the glory of the Lord is going to rise on His people and appear upon them. The final result of this clash between the light and the darkness is that the nations turn to the Lord.

Back to the Future

As we continue this study of prophecy, a look into the future, we will do it from both a biblical and historical perspective. Many of the prophecies from Scripture about the end of this age are now history. These are unfolding at what seems to be an increasingly fast pace. As we can see what has been fulfilled, we can more clearly see what yet must be fulfilled. To understand where we need to go, we must know where we are. To see this outline of history in the Scriptures not only makes the word of prophecy more sure, but it helps us to see where we are in the unfolding plan.

The breakdown in many teachings about the end of the age has been caused by the ignorance of history. Unfortunately, much of the popular eschatology is taught by those who seem to be ignorant of history, so these fulfillments are seldom, if ever, addressed. The result is many are wasting time looking and preparing for things to happen that have already happened. This causes a disconnection with the times and the present purposes of the Lord. What is about to happen is a great disconnection by the church to the fear gripping the world, and a greater connection to the One who has overcome the world and has the answer to every human problem.

Unity Brings Clarity

I am not by this claiming to have the complete picture myself, but I do have some pieces that others seem to be leaving out. We all see in part and know in part, so to have the complete picture, we must put the part that we have together with parts others have been given. The body of Christ will never see clearly or be fully prepared for her purpose until we come together in unity. This unity is beginning to take place in a remarkable way with some. In fact, so much of the groundwork for this has been done it could be that the final unifying of the body could take place almost overnight.

However, in the minds of many, a huge stronghold is hindering them from this, which must be addressed. This one stronghold that is holding back the unity of the body of Christ has been the fear which has perpetrated about the evils and deception of the coming one-world government. It is not wrong to believe in the coming one-world government or one-world currency, but we have let this dominate our vision so that fear of the false has caused us to also reject the true unity that must come to the body of Christ. This exaggerated fear of unity has proven to be far more deceptive and destructive in keeping people from their purposes in the Lord than the actual one-world government will ever be.

Again, we need to understand the evil intention of the devil's counterfeit unity. A true understanding of it will not hinder Christians from coming into the unity that is one of the most basic desires of the Lord's own heart that He expressed in John 17. We must not let a fear of the coming evil unity negate the unity of the body of Christ—this true unity being the only haven from the consequences of the evil that is coming. Christians who are bound together in the Lord in love and unity will not fear the things that the devil is bringing upon the world.

This kind of fear that keeps people from their purpose happens when we spend more time trying to see what the devil is up to rather than trying to see what God is doing. An eschatology based in fear will be deception. Like the text from Isaiah 60 just quoted, the biblical prophecies are clear about the problems and troubles that are coming, and we will be deceived if we cannot see those. We want to prepare for them adequately, but the truth will impart far more faith for the times than fear.

One of the big differences in the coming new order of leadership in the body of Christ will be their ability to see the same events and draw radically different conclusions from them than has been done in the past—just like Joshua and Caleb did. They will not be afraid of the giants in the land, such as a one-world government, or anything else the devil is up to, but they will see the nations as their inheritance in Christ. They will resolve to take those nations for His name sake, by **"the word of His grace" (see Acts 14:3).**

THE INCREASE OF THE KNOWLEDGE OF GOD

More important than knowing where the church is headed is being resolved to be a part of the great host that is going there. A new order is just beginning to awaken to their destiny who will soon be the most powerful spiritual force the world has ever seen. It is your calling if you are alive today to be a part of that great host.

We are in the days of miracles and wonders that will eventually eclipse those of any other time. As we are told in I Corinthians 15:46, **"However, the spiritual is not first, but the natural; then the spiritual."** What has been true in the natural will soon be true in the spiritual realm, so let's take a moment to look at how awesome it has been in the natural, considering this to be a pattern for what is to come spiritually.

The world changed more in the twentieth century than it has in all of previously recorded human history. Knowledge was increasing at a rate so fast that by the middle of the twentieth century more knowledge

49

was gained each year than in any previous century. Then the end of the twentieth century, knowledge was increasing so fast that more knowledge was being gained every week than in any previous century. As stunning as this is, the great increase of knowledge is still accelerating.

Knowledge is now increasing so fast that the half-life of many technical degrees is only eighteen months, and yet it takes four or more years to get them. Education is beginning to fall behind the increase of knowledge, with some estimates that even the best universities were running years behind cutting-edge knowledge. Other schools are now running decades behind. Of course, these universities deny this, but even the discoveries that are made on their own campuses can take many years to get into the classrooms. Change is now coming almost too fast to see, much less to understand or incorporate into schools.

Just a few centuries ago astronomy leaped ahead when we went from seeing the earth as flat, and the center of the universe that everything revolved around, to being just one of a number of planets that actually revolved around the sun. Then the sun was perceived to be a rather small star among millions of others. Then it was just one of billions in our galaxy. The Milky Way, which soon was understood to be just one of billions of other galaxies, is made up of billions of stars. Then the discovery of the "red shift" proved that the universe was expanding, fast! Like our perception of the universe, knowledge has been increasing at a rate that was incomprehensible just decades ago.

Universities gave birth to this great increase of knowledge, and like mothers who die in childbirth, they may actually be doomed by what they have given birth to. Universities were truly a remarkable development for mankind, and they have been the engine for most of the great advances we have made in knowledge. However, by the end of the twentieth century, corporations on the cutting-edge of technology were declaring that they would no longer hire college graduates because the system of teaching rewarded mediocrity and inhibited the creativity and original thinking that were needed to operate in such a fast-changing environment. So the very system of education that had more than any other entity prepared the world for the times was now threatening to become a victim of the times. Industries and even individual corporations are now considering starting their own schools that teach students to think "outside the box" in a way that they will have to if they are going to be able to function in these times.

What does this have to do with us as Christians? The great increase of knowledge that has come in the natural is about to come in the spiritual realm. This increase of the knowledge of God and His ways is going to release a supernatural force that will walk in dominion over the natural realm like has never been done before. However, the church in its present form will not be able to keep up with the pace of change that is coming. The church is about to morph into a form so radically different that many Christians will have a hard time recognizing it. Those who do will be

51

a part of the future and must learn to embrace and even thrive with fast-paced change. The dwelling place of the Creator will become the most exciting, creative, powerful force on the earth. What is coming cannot be contained in much of our rigid, institutional thinking. The veil of the temple is about to be rent again, and God in all of His dynamic glory will be revealed openly to the people, through His people. More will be said about this later, but we must be able to embrace change or we will be swept away by what is coming.

The Most Valuable Commodity

To the prophetically gifted, these times are not confusing, but are increasingly exhilarating. Again, as we are told in Acts 2:17, **"And it shall come to pass in the last days, says God, that I will pour out of My Spirit on all flesh; your sons and your daughters shall prophesy, your young men shall see visions, your old men shall dream dreams"** (NKJV). This includes young and old, male and female, which covers everyone. We are told that this will happen in **"the last days,"** when the Lord pours out His Spirit. We can expect that at the end of this age all of God's people will have prophetic experiences and gifts.

I submit that the Greek word for **"all"** in this text could have been translated "whole," and the word for **"flesh"** could have been translated "body," so this text could have been translated "whole body." It is a wrong interpretation to think that the Lord is going to pour out His Spirit on all people or "all mankind" as some have translated this, because we are told in the next verse that this will come upon "His bondservants" (see Acts 2:18). However, believe it or not, like it or not, all of God's people are going to be empowered by the Holy Spirit, and the result of this is going to be these prophetic experiences coming upon all. The effect of this infusion of revelation upon God's people will be a great clarity about the times as well as each one being prepared for them. Prophecy has been the heritage of God's people since the beginning, and it will be until the end of the age. In the age to come, it will obviously no longer be needed, but at the end of this one, we will need it more than ever.

Corporations are trying to teach their thinkers to see into the future and at increasing distances. There are Japanese companies that have five-hundred year plans. They are not only thinking that far ahead, but planning that far ahead. That is impressive, but the Lord gave us a one-thousand year plan, and it is absolute and will come to pass. This plan will become increasingly clear, but what we also need is clarity about next year, even next month. That too is available to those who seek it, which we are encouraged to do in I Corinthians 14:1, **"Pursue love, yet desire earnestly spiritual gifts, but especially that you may prophesy."**

I am a great lover of education and the whole principle of universities, but I know that those who do not discern the times and make some profound changes to get in line with them will not be with us much longer. Even those with the greatest names and largest endowments can pass away fast. We are in "the information age," and information is now more valuable than any other commodity, including monetary endowments. Trustworthy prophetic gifts are more valuable than any other form of knowledge because knowledge of the future trumps the value of any other kind of knowledge. Take a moment to think about the value of what the Lord has given to His church, and as we just read from Acts 2, this will come upon all of His people **"in the last days."**

In the natural, businesses that cannot foresee trends and prepare for them are finding it increasingly difficult to just survive, much less prosper. More and more great companies that had been household names just a few years ago have vanished fast, simply because they could not change fast enough, or they made the fatal mistake of making the wrong changes. In releasing this unprecedented increase of knowledge, mankind has also released forces that will become increasingly beyond man's ability to control, at least in our present state that is disconnected from God. In the natural, if you cannot see prophetically into the future, you will be an endangered company or university. Seeing into the future is vital for survival.

As stated, what has been happening in the natural is now beginning to happen in the spiritual. Spiritual knowledge is beginning to increase at a similar, dramatic pace as natural knowledge. For Christianity, the twentieth century was like no other. From the beginning of that century, moves of God came like great tsunami waves across the world. Each one was radically changing the spiritual coastlines of the world. Though the basic doctrines of the faith have not changed and cannot change, church life has and is changing dramatically and fundamentally. It needed to for the church to be relevant to the times and accomplish her purpose in them.

Like the universities that helped prepare the way for the great increase of knowledge in the natural, the great church institutions that have helped prepare the way for these times spiritually may go on operating for some time, but they are falling further and further behind and the people in them more and more out of touch. Awakenings and renewals will be sent from God to help them, and those who begin to move with Him cannot only survive, but be transformed into great resources for the advancing church. However, the ability to embrace change will be required for survival.

In contrast to this, like some of the dominant industries to emerge in the last few decades that were begun in garages by college dropouts, some of the most powerful Christian movements now emerging were started in the most humble, unexpected places, by those who have not spent a day in a seminary. Even so, they are changing the face of the church like no seminary has ever done.

The Currency of the Future is Change

I am a strong believer in seminaries, and they have a very important role to play in helping to keep the church moored to sound biblical doctrine, especially in these fast-paced times. However, like universities, many seminaries are falling behind the times, and the ones that cannot make the needed radical changes for the future will also pass away. However, there is good evidence that these changes can and will be made by some; therefore we should not give up on any for as long as there is life in them.

I am also a local church man. True Christian maturity and the fulfillment of our purpose as individuals is simply not possible without a strong and vital local church life. True Christianity was designed that way by its founder, Christ Jesus Himself. Local church life as it was designed to be almost two thousand years ago is the most brilliant, relevant, and powerful force that has ever been seen on the earth. What it was distracted into being for much of the intervening centuries is a big difference from the way it was designed, but the truth, life, and power of the local church is beginning to emerge again. It will be the most powerful force on the earth. That, too, is a sure biblical prophecy and it will surely come to pass.

Likewise, I have a very high regard for all that the great church institutions have accomplished and the strong moorings they have given, not only to Christianity but to society. Out of a love and respect for them I write and say all that I do, hoping to help them discern the times and make all the necessary changes to be a part of them. They can still play an important part and be a huge help for what is unfolding. However, those who do not discern the times and flow with them will not be with us much longer—they will be washed away in the waves of change that are coming.

The church and church life have changed and are continuing to change at a rapid pace. The changes that are coming are from the Lord and are proceeding toward Him. They are preparing His people for the greatest move of the Spirit in human history—the last move of God of the age. However, many of the radical changes we are experiencing are simply a return to what was given to the church in the beginning—the brilliance and simplicity of the family of God as we were intended to relate together. True church is a family, not just an organization. When we start becoming an organization instead of a family, we cease to be the true church. Family is the incubator of life, in the natural and spiritual.

True Discernment

The exhortation from I Corinthians14:1 that was noted previously—to earnestly desire spiritual gifts and especially prophecy—began with **"pursue love."** Love is not possible without relationship. The reason why family is under the greatest assault of the devil in our times is because it is the most powerful force, and therefore a threat to his domain of darkness. Christians, who grow in the power, authority, and knowledge of the times, will be growing in love, and therefore their relationships will be getting stronger in their families and in their churches. Without love, accurate knowledge is not possible, as we are told in Philippians 1:9-10:

And this I pray, that your love may abound still more and more in real knowledge and all discernment,

> **so that you may approve the things that are excellent, in order to be sincere and blameless until the day of Christ;**

As we are told here, love must be abounding for **"real knowledge"** and **"all discernment."** The most important thing we can do, and the basic job description of every Christian, is to love God. True Christian maturity can be measured by how much our love for Him is growing. If we love Him as we should, we will also love others as we should. Without that love, all knowledge and all discernment will be distorted. As our knowledge increases, let us be even more resolute to not be beguiled and led astray from the simplicity of devotion to Christ (see II Corinthians 11:3), and from the most basic calling that we all have—to love God and one another.

With the incredible increase of knowledge in the natural, it seems that the universe is getting bigger in dramatic leaps. Of course, it has always been big; we are just discovering how big it is. In the other direction, looking at small things, like cells and atoms, our knowledge was likewise increasing. With the discovery of DNA, the Theory of Evolution instantly began to look as foolish as the perception that the world was flat. However, because there is no other theory available that does not eliminate God from the equation, many scientists have done their best to hold on to the Theory of Evolution, but it has only looked more and more ridiculous with each attempt. This has made the religion of science begin to look as silly as the theologians who tried to hang on to the "world is flat" concept after it was so blatantly disproven. However, in physics and astronomy, some of the most notable scientists, who were also agnostic or even atheists, have been confessing publicly how irrational their previous thinking has been.

The fact of intelligent design is so overwhelmingly obvious that we can expect every true scientist, who is devoted to truth in their profession, to acknowledge this if they have not already. The last to hold out against this groundswell will only prolong the most ridiculous. Almost every new discovery points at intelligent design.

Two Witnesses

I am not saying that these are *the two* witnesses in the Book of Revelation, but true religion and true science should be best friends. They remarkably confirm one another, and believe it or not, they are moving in that direction now. As Jon Amos Comenius once said, "Nature is God's second book," which is kind of a paraphrase of what Paul wrote in the first chapter of Romans. The discoveries of science are more and more declaring the ways and nature of God and His plan. Without the Holy Spirit, the Spirit of truth, scientists cannot make the connection of Who God really is, but we can, and we can be edified by their work.

Many on both sides, science and religion, are still fighting about coming closer together, but it is inevitable, and almost every profound new discovery has started confirming the biblical testimony, when it is translated accurately. True religion will set science ultimately free from the shackles of trying to fit everything into the Theory of Evolution that increasingly makes distortions of the facts necessary.

This deserves more attention than I can give it here, and there are others who are much more qualified in both science and theology who are doing it much better than I could. I am simply trying to make the point that we must not fear the increase of knowledge in the natural or spiritual.

The discovery of the universe as it is does not in any way conflict with the biblical record, and true theologians should never be threatened by the discovery of the universe as it is. As Jon Amos Comenius also prophesied in the early 1600s, all true science will lead to the Creator, and all true scientific discoveries are pointing to Him more and more boldly. The concept that the universe just evolved on its own with millions of random accidents happening in perfect timing is no longer acceptable to any rational thinker.

So What Do We Do?

Christians have been entrusted with the most powerful weapons in the world—love, truth, and accurate knowledge of the future. We are going to be given these in increasing quantities, but we need to keep them in the proper order. We will learn how to use them together effectively to prepare the way for the coming of the Lord. As we are told in Isaiah 40, the way we do this is to build a highway. This highway will join heaven and earth so that heaven can come to the earth.

The education system did so much to ignite the great increase of knowledge that the world is now experiencing. However, it has started becoming too rigid and inflexible to keep up with the fast changes it helped to release so many of the great institutions of Christianity find themselves in the same predicament. They must make radical changes or they will continue to fade away as archaic relics of the past, instead of being a force of great power and influence as they have been.

Even so, resistance to change is not always a bad thing. A healthy resistance to new knowledge can help to purify that knowledge. However, there is a difference in challenging something to prove the truth of it, and challenging anything new and different out of the fear of change or just self-preservation. Those who have been motivated by the latter have inevitably passed away and needed to. Those who are motivated by the former are true shepherds and watchmen and deserve continued influence.

Change is coming with increasing speed. However, we do not just want change but the right change. The sure word of prophecy gives us a clear path into the future, and we want to be sure that all changes we accept keep us on that path, which is the highway that the kingdom of God is going to come on.

To help build that highway is the most noble cause, and its completion will be the greatest achievement of this age. It is being paved with "living stones" whose lives will fit together in a symmetry that no mere human engineering could ever achieve. Spiritual engineering is done spiritually with love, truth, peace, patience, kindness, and so on.

The new order will build their lives on an unyielding devotion to truth and a resolution of heart that will never compromise the truth or yield even an acre of ground to its enemies. They will be at the same time a highway, a temple, an army, and a bride, with all of these blending into the most remarkable force the world has ever seen so that no place on earth will be able to escape their message.

In these first chapters, I have been laying a groundwork of concepts, and the coming chapters will be more practical and specific. These concepts are necessary to understand the times and how we must fit into them. Everything is changing, but we serve a God who never changes! As everything in this world begins to ebb and flow, sometimes in sporadic and uncontrolled directions, we have a Rock, and we are all called to stand solidly upon Him, resolutely committed to following Him, so that we can help give light in the darkness to show the way. To be this light, we must know where we are going.

THE TREASURE MAP

The greatest treasure found on this earth is the Holy Spirit. The Holy Spirit is "God with us," whom He has given to live in those who obey Him. The Holy Spirit will lead us to Jesus, lead us into all truth, and convict us of sin when we need it. He is the Helper, the Comforter, and seeks **"the deep things of God" (see I Corinthians 2:10)**, compelling those who are "Spirit filled" to do the same. God Himself is the greatest treasure, and the pursuit of God is the ultimate quest that we can have in this life.

Those who are in pursuit of God also have an inheritance in Him, which is a specific calling, a land that is a sphere of authority that we are called to take dominion over in His name. Therefore, to do His will, and to accomplish this, is the true measure of a successful life. The Bible affirms that God knew us before the foundation of the world and called us with a purpose. To find this purpose, this inheritance, so we can fulfill it is the great treasure we will now discuss. To find it and accomplish it is the ultimate fulfillment that we can have in life. Because we were created for a purpose, we will never have true peace or satisfaction until we find it and fulfill it. All other pursuits will ultimately prove vain and empty but this one.

To perceive our individual purpose begins with seeing the overall plan of God. Only when we see this clearly will we be able to see where we fit into it clearly. Neither are easy because if they were this would not be a treasure. What makes something valuable is that it is either rare or hard to get. The true kings of this earth, who will rule and reign with Christ, take the challenge and are on a life quest to find and do His will.

The Map

The most clear and specific biblical model or map of where we are now in history is the Book of Joshua and the conquest of the Promised Land by Israel. This was intended to be a map for us as we are told in I Corinthians 10, where the major events of Israel's journey are retold in an outline form. **"Now these things happened to them as an example, and they were written for our instruction, upon whom the ends of the ages have come" (I Corinthians 10:11).**

Everything that happened to Israel was recorded and passed down in the Scriptures for us. This is what the Lord Jesus meant when He said, **"The Law prophesied" (see Matthew 11:13).** By looking back and knowing history, we can see an amazing prophecy and outline of church history in the events that happened with Israel. When we start to see that all of these things were written thousands of years before for us, for our instruction at the end of this age, it gives us great boldness in our purpose. It is an outline that shows us where we are, where we must go next, and where our ultimate goal is. It also gives us a general timing.

I use the word "general" here because prophecy is almost always general—specific enough to give us confidence in it, but general enough to make us need the Holy Spirit as our guide. We can know all of this in great detail, but we are still compelled to follow the Lord. It is a brilliance far beyond any human ingenuity and in all ways and always it seeks to work out the ultimate purpose of God, which is the reconciliation of man to Him in the closest possible relationship.

In all ways and always, this closeness to Him is far better than the Promised Land that we are seeking to possess. Therefore, the journey, the battles, and even the setbacks and mistakes, are to be treasured as ways to get closer to Him, know Him better, and know His ways better. Closeness to God will always be far better than any earthly treasure or inheritance.

When we receive an earthly inheritance, it is almost always after the death of our parents or relations. It is not so with our spiritual inheritance. We receive it from One who will live forever, and we receive it as one more thing in which we can relate to Him and get closer to Him. This is why we are told in II Corinthians

1:20, **"For as many as may be the promises of God, in Him they are yes."** We do not inherit apart from Him but rather as a part of Him and His body.

As we study Israel's conquest of their Promised Land, how this relates to us, and how the church is going to walk in all of the promises of God, let us always keep in mind that as wonderful as they all are, and as wonderful as our citizenship in heaven is, the greatest inheritance of all is the King Himself.

The Path

Every detail of Israel's experience of crossing over into the Promised Land, and how they fought and succeeded in taking it, has prophetic significance for us. The Lord chose the path and the sequence of the battles for a purpose. The wilderness experience was intended to deliver the people from their slave nature, to prepare them for the battles ahead, which were to prepare them for reigning over their inheritance in a way that would make it a witness and a representation of the kingdom of God.

As Israel first looked across the Jordan River at their Promised Land, they could not help but see what appeared to be two impregnable obstacles—the Jordan River itself, which was overflowing all of its banks, and then Jericho, possibly the most powerful stronghold of all. Likely, they were all thinking that they would like to just start with a few little villages first. However, the Lord wanted them to learn at the very beginning that just as they needed Him to make it through the wilderness, they needed Him to possess their inheritance too. He wanted them to know from the beginning that even though they were going to have to fight for their inheritance, they still needed Him. After every great victory, they would not trust more in themselves but in Him. They would have to fight for their inheritance so that they would value it, but their inheritance could not take precedence over Him in their lives or it would be a stumbling block instead of a blessing.

Both the biblical and historic testimonies make it clear that anything attained too fast or too easily is almost always insignificant. We can see this in the lives of everyone who accomplished great things for God. The kind of preparation they went through reflected the significance of their calling. We must get one important fact in our hearts right now—the Lord does not want it to be easy, He wants it to be impossible!

The U.S. Navy Construction Battalions (CBs) have a motto, "The difficult we do immediately. The impossible takes a little longer." That should be the church's motto. The Lord wanted Israel to start with the impossible to show them right away that there is nothing impossible for Him. That is the mentality that we must have if we are going to possess our Promised Land. This is not about our abilities or inabilities, but about the One who is leading us. What He has called us to do He will empower us to do. This is the mentality of faith that we must have from the very beginning. Those who look at themselves will fear. Those who look to Him will believe. We must keep our eyes on Him.

Many Christians struggle their entire lives in confusion about whether they should fight the battles or let the Lord fight them, and the answer is that both are true. In just a couple of cases in Scripture, the Lord told Israel to stand and watch His salvation, but the rest of the time they fought and He fought with them. It is amazing how many have seized on the couple of isolated examples to base their mode of operation while neglecting the rest of the Scriptures. Even if the Lord calls us to stand and watch His salvation, it is not likely that this is what He will call us to do again.

When His people were obedient to Him, they almost always had to fight, and He would supply what they lacked, which meant that sometimes He powerfully and miraculously defeated their enemies, but He still required them to go out and face the enemy. Of course, the weapons of our warfare are not carnal, and our fight is not like Israel's, but it is a fight. We must learn to resist the enemy if he is going to flee from us. We must learn to stand up against evil, injustice, and the unrighteousness that is prevailing over our inheritance.

The Lord is called "the Lord of hosts," which means "Lord of armies," more than ten times more than all of His other titles. He is a martial God, and His people are called to be an army. We are called to be both worshipers and warriors, and these two natures do not conflict with each other. This is why one of the greatest worshipers in Scripture, King David, was also one of the greatest warriors. He is the one about whom it is also said that he was a man after God's own heart.

He fought the battles of the Lord and was actually the only one in Israel's history who fully took all of the land that Israel was to have as an inheritance.

The path into the Promised Land is hard because God intended for it to be hard. What we are called to inherit is not cheap, and those who inherit it will be those who value it enough to fight for it. For this reason, there will be a military demeanor to come upon the body of Christ, a martial resolve to fight for what is right and for the inheritance of the Lord.

The generation that perished in the wilderness was born in slavery and they could not get free from the slave mentality. The first few times they faced conflict, they proved even willing to go back into slavery rather than to fight. The generation that takes the land will not have been born into slavery, and they will have the demeanor of warriors like Joshua and Caleb who led Israel into the Promised Land.

As stated, much of the last-day battle between light and darkness will be between fear and faith. If we are controlled by fear, then fear is our lord. Those who follow the Lord will not be controlled by fear but by faith. They will be of the nature of David who when all of Israel was intimidated by one giant, did not just see big giant, he saw a giant that was a target so big he would be hard to miss!

The emerging generation will not be content to hide within the walls of church buildings. They will not endure boring meetings, knowing deep in their souls that a true walk with God is the most exciting adventure we can know in this life. The emerging generation will not be content with a powerless message, but will know they cannot be true witnesses of an almighty God without power. They will also reject any form of worship that denies His power. They will not be content to just read the stories about the great things that He has done, they will want to see Him do great things through them, and they will see it.

From Death Will Come Life

In recent years, earthquakes, tsunamis, and storms have been taxing the whole world's relief efforts. We can expect these kinds of disasters to not only continue but increase. This is not a negative prophecy—it is a biblical prophecy. This is the result of the creation groaning and travailing for mankind to return to his rightful place and rule over the earth as God originally commissioned him to do. This travail will increase until the kingdom comes. The destructive nature of it will exceed all human remedy, but it will not even tax the resources of the kingdom.

The world's health experts are expecting the Avian, or "bird flu," to potentially become the most devastating plague in world history. Even though it may not have been in the news for a while, this deadly plague is moving relentlessly toward the place where it mutates into what can be transferred human to human. When that happens, it will be beyond what even the entire world's health officials can cope with, and it will be a matter of governments just trying to keep order in the midst of the devastation.

Government leaders have been very wise in their restraint in the way that they have let out information about this, not wanting to cause a panic, yet preparing to take quick and decisive action when it comes. I have personally questioned authorities and they believe the death toll could be hundreds of millions, even billions. One even said they thought that it could be the biblical plague from the Book of Revelation that kills one-third of mankind. They all agree that it is not a matter of if it will come, but when.

When I inquired of the Lord if this were true, He confirmed it to me in a dream. He also showed how we could be completely safe from it. The body of Christ must get this in our hearts right now—we do not have to be subject to the things that are coming upon the rest of the world. Like Israel in Goshen, when the plagues were poured out on Egypt, the Lord is going to make a distinction between His people and those who do not obey Him.

Why are we talking about this as we are discussing taking our land, our inheritance? In Scripture, the Jordan River often represents death. The Lord said that **"the harvest is the end of the age" (see Matthew 13:39),** and we read that **"the Jordan overflows all its banks all the days of harvest" (see Joshua 3:15).** This speaks of how death will be overflowing *all* of its banks *all* of the days of the harvest, which is the end of this age.

Because of this, we can expect natural disasters and human disasters to increase during the coming times. However, we should not have fear about any of this, but rather rejoice that our salvation is drawing near. It is time to cross over and possess our inheritance.

No Christian should be afraid of death. Death is swallowed up in victory for us. Death is the door to heaven and should be willingly embraced by all Christians when it is our time. Regardless of how good our lives are here, we should be like Paul was about this, wanting to stay and have more fruit, but even more wanting to go and be with the Lord.

Even though we should not have a fear of death, Christians should not be dying with cancer and other diseases. This is not to condemn anyone who is afflicted with a disease, but it is a reflection of the low state of spiritual authority that we have in the church at this time because this is happening to our people. This will change, but until it does, even if we or a loved one is passing with one of these diseases, we should, above all people, die well. We should not be hearing the questions from doctors and nurses about why Christians do not die better than others do, but we should hear testimonies marveling at how well every Christian dies in peace because they are entering the door to glory. If we really believe the gospel, how can we not be excited when our day comes?

Of course, having not faced that day myself yet, I don't really know how well I will do either; however, the thought of it is not a dread to me, but exciting. The last time someone checked, I think the mortality rate was hovering somewhere around 100 percent. It is inevitable that we all die, except the few who are remaining when the Lord comes. Why not resolve to demonstrate the ultimate faith when confronted with the ultimate fear, the fear of death? Having known a few Christians who crossed over and physically died and were somehow brought back, I have never met one that wanted to come back.

If we die because we do not have the victory over a disease or get into an accident, this in no way cancels our eternal salvation. To walk in what we are called to walk in through the coming times, we must get free of the fear of death, which we do by going to the cross every day, dying daily as Paul said, by not loving our lives even to the death (see I Corinthians 15:31). We are called to be dead to this world. What can the world possibly do to a dead man? A dead man has no more fear of any kind. Those who live lives that are dead to this world will be the most alive people in this world. Those who become the slaves of Christ will be the most free.

No Fear

When we bought the former Heritage Grand Hotel and Conference Center (also known as PTL), we had massive renovations to do. When we were finally able to open some of the rooms, our first Certificate of Occupancy was for 91 rooms. At our first water baptism at Heritage, 91 people were baptized. The first time we prayed for people to receive the baptism in the Holy

Spirit at Heritage, 91 people responded. Even when I shared with the congregation that the Lord was obviously speaking to us about Psalm 91, the power on the battery of my laptop was 91 percent. In too many ways to recount here, the Lord has continued to inculcate Psalm 91 to us as a crucial message for these times. Take the time to read it, slowly. I have quoted it below for your convenience.

> He who dwells in the shelter of the Most High will abide in the shadow of the Almighty.
>
> I will say to the Lord, "My refuge and my fortress, my God, in whom I trust!"
>
> For it is He who delivers you from the snare of the trapper, and from the deadly pestilence.
>
> He will cover you with His pinions, and under His wings you may seek refuge; His faithfulness is a shield and bulwark.
>
> You will not be afraid of the terror by night, or of the arrow that flies by day;
>
> Of the pestilence that stalks in darkness, or of the destruction that lays waste at noon.
>
> A thousand may fall at your side, and ten thousand at your right hand; *but* it shall not approach you.
>
> You will only look on with your eyes, and see the recompense of the wicked.

For you have made the Lord, my refuge, *even* the Most High, your dwelling place.

No evil will befall you, nor will any plague come near your tent.

For He will give His angels charge concerning you, to guard you in all your ways.

They will bear you up in their hands, lest you strike your foot against a stone.

You will tread upon the lion and cobra, the young lion and the serpent you will trample down.

"Because he has loved Me, therefore I will deliver him; I will set him *securely* on high, because he has known My name.

"He will call upon Me, and I will answer him; I will be with him in trouble; I will rescue him, and honor him.

"With a long life I will satisfy him, and let him behold My salvation."

There are a couple of points I would like to highlight here. This **"snare of the trapper"** sounds a bit like the "bird flu," doesn't it? Fowlers are ones who keep birds, especially chickens, which have been the most susceptible to this plague so far. Of course, the biggest threat will be when it mutates so that it is transferred from human to human. When that happens, it will spread worldwide, and fast, some saying in as little as four days. Those who are hearing the words of the Lord and obeying them will be prepared for this, and it will be one of the greatest opportunities in history for the gospel.

Psalm 91 also states that having a thousand fall on one side and ten thousand on the other, but it will not come near us. It may not be as much fun to talk about this now, but we must if we are going to be prepared. The worst thing that could happen to us is that we get the bird flu, die, and go to heaven. We can't lose! The worst thing that can happen to us is so wonderful that there should be no room for fear. There is simply no place on earth more safe for us than being in God's will, even if that is standing in the midst of such a plague.

What I was shown in the dream, which confirmed that this plague was indeed coming, was that those who are in their right place in His body would be safe. The way we would get into the right place in His body is by using the "key of the kingdom," which is making all major decisions by seeking the kingdom first, not just following our own will and desires.

One who is seeking the kingdom first would never make a major decision on where the best job is, the geography they liked the best, or even being the closest to friends and family, but they would make such decisions on where the Lord wants them placed in His body, the church.

We cannot be properly connected to the Head without also being properly connected to His body, the church. As Paul wrote in I Corinthians 11, it is for this reason (not discerning the Lord's body) that many are weak, sick, sleep, or die prematurely.

Like it or not, believe it or not, rebellious, self-willed Christians will suffer the judgments more severely than the heathen who do not know the truth. That is biblical, and we will address it in a bit more detail later, but that should not concern us unless we are rebellious or have loved ones who are, in which case it should compel us to warn them to come to their senses.

If we have fear as we read of the things coming upon the world, obviously we are not right with the Lord in some vital ways, and this is the opportunity to get right. Repentance changes everything. Even if we are far from the will of God because we have not used the key of the kingdom, and have made major decisions on our own preferences rather than seeking His will first, if we repent He will help us to get us back on the right path. As C.S. Lewis once observed, "In the Lord the wrong path never becomes the right path." If we are on the wrong path, the only way to get on the right one is to go back to where we missed the turn, and make the right choice.

This could mean that if we are living in the wrong place, we may need to move. It could mean leaving our job, families, and other things that we love. However, our lives will be measurably better, if not longer, if we do this. He promises that if we use the key to the kingdom, seeking His kingdom first, and putting His interests first in all that we do, He will take care of everything else that we need. He can do this much better than we can. If we do our part, He will do His part, and that is the best deal we will ever get in this life.

One of the primary ways that we can know if we are in the right place is by the way we fit into the local body, the church. When people say to me that there is no church close to them that they feel at home in, I know right away that this is likely because they are living in the wrong place. This is almost always the result of them not using the "key of the kingdom" in making such major decisions as where they live, where they work, where they send their kids to school.

If you are wondering why your life is so hard and everything seems so disjointed, it is most likely because you are disjointed, not in the right place in His body. As Paul wrote, this causes weakness, sickness, and even premature death.

After choosing to give our lives to the Lord and choosing our spouse, the most important decision we will likely make is the local church that we will be a part of. This will only be taken lightly by those who take the Lord and His purposes lightly. The Lord promises that if we seek we will find, and this is something that needs to be a top priority until we find where we are supposed to be. Now it is important, but in due time it will be life or death.

Many are falling to the deadly teaching that having a coffee with some Christian friends is all the church life you need—that is a lie that will take many lives in the times to come. Even if that is a preference of many Christians today who feel disconnected from the present church, it is not the preference of Christians who make something a truth, even the preference of a majority of Christians, but it is what the Lord says is truth. In Scripture, all who came to the Lord were added to the church. They found their place; they fit into it and grew in their purpose as the church grew.

If all of the disconnected Christians were in their right places, they would not feel so disconnected and out of step with where the church is because the church would likely be much further along than she is with the vision, zeal, and life that the presently disconnected ones would have brought to her. This can be rationalized in many ways, but we will not fulfill our own purpose in this life without being rightly related to a local body of believers. We will not mature spiritually as we should without all of the frustrations, problems, and other opportunities to grow in love, faith, and the rest of the fruit of the Spirit that we are given in the local church.

When Israel pulled up to the Jordan River, everyone knew their tribe, the place of their family in the tribe, and their places in their family. They were in order. They were in what is called "martial array." There were no drifters or floaters among them, but they knew their places and were in them. That is what the church is about to look like because we are drawing near to the Jordan River and the fight for our Promised Land.

THE DOOR TO THE KINGDOM

As all of the Lord Jesus' own prophecies concerning these times make clear, we are coming to the greatest times of trouble the world has ever known. The good news is, if we have built our lives on the kingdom which cannot be shaken, we will not only survive what is coming, but we will prevail and prosper right through them. This is actually the time when the church is going to cross over and begin to possess its Promised Land. We are told in Acts 14:22, **"Through many tribulations we must enter the kingdom of God."** Through what has been popularly referred to as "the great tribulation" at the end of this age, the whole world will enter into the kingdom of God. Our redemption is drawing near!

We are headed for very difficult times, but they will not be for those who are living in the kingdom. We are told in Daniel 11:32, **"but the people who know their God will display strength and take action."** The Lord called us to live in this time for a purpose, and we have a job to do. That is what this study is about.

However, the basis of a godly character which we have been studying is critical if we are to prevail in these times.

Because death will be overflowing **"all its banks"** during **"all the days of the harvest" (see Joshua 3:15)**, we must prepare ourselves for increasingly great natural and manmade disasters as we get closer to the end of this age. Again, we will need to learn to cope with death all around us and keep on functioning. Just as no general is likely to be successful if he is overly-concerned about casualties, we, too, will have to learn to cope with death on all sides, not being overly-given to grieving or mourning the dead, in order to save the living from an even greater, eternal disaster.

Again, the prophecies of these times will only be fearful for those who are not abiding in the Prince of Peace. Such fear is evidence of not coming to abide in Him which should be a wake-up call to those who do not. We must understand the problems that are coming if we are going to be prepared for them. Actually, a good case could be made that the world has never had as many troubles and been surrounded by so many dangers as we are right now. To avoid looking for them because they make us uncomfortable or fearful is to live in deception. Those who have built their lives on the kingdom have nothing to fear. Those who have not built their lives on the kingdom have much to fear, and it is better for them to fear now than to go on in their delusions and remain in the terrible jeopardy those delusions keep them in. Therefore, we want to see these things for what they are and be prepared, not just to survive but to save others.

Save the People

Israel's inheritance was the land, and they dispossessed the people who were on it. Our inheritance, which is also the Lord's, is the people. The power of His indestructible life will be flowing through us to reap the greatest harvest that the world has ever known. We must not sleep or be distracted while the treasure of the earth is ripe for reaping.

The Lord made it clear in His Word: If we are to partake of His life we must also partake of His death **"that they who live should no longer live for themselves, but for Him" (see II Corinthians 5:15)**. Any other teaching is a false gospel and an enemy of the cross. Death separates the things that are natural from the things that are spiritual. To have a resurrection, there must first be a death. If we want to walk in the resurrection life of Jesus, we must be willing to lay down our lives for Him.

As we touched on before, death is the greatest liberation that we can ever know. If we are dead to this world there is nothing the world can do to us. It is impossible for a dead man to have a fear of failure, fear of rejection, or even fear of the dark. To the degree that any fear still has its grip on us is only to the degree that we have failed to go to the cross. The cross will set us free from all fear!

A dead man does not lust, covet, feel anger, want to get revenge, or even feel lonely. There is no freedom that we can ever have greater than that which comes from dying to this world so as to be alive to Christ. The cross does not just represent death, but the door to resurrection life. We must die to this present world, this present age, so we can begin to live now in the age to come.

The cross is the power of God, and those who want to walk in His power in their daily lives will learn to take up their crosses daily. Those who do so will become free from all of the yokes of this present evil age and will walk in a freedom and boldness greater than has been seen on the earth on such a scale for nearly two thousand years. When the great Christian mystics arose each day, resolving to seek and do the will of the Lord rather than seek their own interests, they experienced a joy and peace the world simply could not understand.

Save the Nations

The Great Commission was to make disciples of all nations, not just individuals. We also see that when the Lord returns He is going to divide the nations into sheep and goats, not just individuals. Right now, it is being decided which nations will be "sheep" and which will be "goats." This does not mean that we should abandon the gospel of salvation, which is basically the way that nations will be changed—by saving and teaching individuals the ways of the Lord. However, we must begin to develop national and international strategies that will impact nations with the gospel, not just a few individuals.

This will, to a large degree, be a major shift in our missionary thinking and strategies, which has actually been happening in some groups over the last two decades or more. There are also some differences in where the church is now and where it was in the first century that we need to understand. Many foundational things will also never change and will always be a basic part of the church's vision and purpose, but there are also some differences at the end of the age. There is a prophecy of this in how Joshua instructed Israel:

> **"However, there shall be between you and it a distance of about 2,000 cubits by measure. Do not come near it, that you may know the way by which you shall go, for you have not passed this way before"** (Joshua 3:4).

Those who follow the Ark, which represents the Lord, by **"about 2,000 cubits,"** which prophetically represents years, will be going a different way than the church has gone before. Many things are the same but many are not, and we need to understand the differences.

The Gospel of the Kingdom

Before the end of this age can come, the gospel of the kingdom must be preached throughout the entire world. This has not yet been done. Until now we have basically preached the gospel of salvation, which is fundamentally the gospel of how we get out of Egypt, which was accomplished by the Passover. This is essential, and it will continue to be the banner of the cross that we march under, always preaching the gospel of individual salvation, but we will also begin to preach the gospel of the kingdom—the kingdom of God is at hand! The King is coming, and He's coming to take over. He is sending us before Him to prepare His way.

In the baptism represented by the Red Sea crossing (see I Corinthians 10:1-2), the Israelites were being chased by their enemies. However, the baptism represented by the crossing of the Jordan began their pursuit of their enemies. This was not just because the circumstances had changed, but because the people had also changed during their long sojourn in the wilderness.

Likewise, the church has seemingly wandered in the wilderness for nearly two thousand years. Just like with Israel's trek through their wilderness, this time was not wasted. A great transformation has been taking place in the people. It was one thing to get the people out of Egypt, but it took much longer to get the Egypt out of them. Likewise, there is a people who may have been just seemingly drifting through life rather aimlessly, but God has been doing a deep work in their hearts, and this time has not been wasted. They are a people prepared for the great challenges ahead that will prepare the way for the coming of the kingdom of God.

From Defense to Offense

The change we must go through will come from a life that has been seemingly composed of being chased and harassed by the devil, and then enduring the deep dealings of God in our own hearts, to the mentality of a conqueror. This does not mean that we are now perfect, but the conquest ahead will help to continue the work on our characters. Even so, there will be a great difference in the conflict—instead of battling the enemies within who have kept us in bondage, we will begin battling the ones without who are keeping others in bondage.

We must always keep in mind that our conquest is not the pursuit of personal gain and advancement, but our treasure is the liberation of souls that are now in the bondage of darkness. These will be our treasures in heaven, laid up for us eternally. Our purpose is to see the truth of the gospel of Jesus Christ set the captives free. We are called as true freedom fighters. Our successes in this life will be counted by the release of the captives that the devil has had in bondage.

We can now expect a big change to begin to take place in the church from just seeking to be set free ourselves, to setting the nations free. On the other side of the Jordan, Israel may not have looked very different from the group who had left Egypt, but on the inside they were very different. They were no longer just recently released slaves—they were conquerors! Right now, by appearances the church may not look very different than it has for many centuries—but it is! We are no longer just recently released slaves—we are warriors with the greatest cause, preparing for the greatest battle.

Some of the greatest revivals and spiritual advances in the history of the church have been taking place over the last two decades. With some of these, whole regions are being transformed and whole nations are being impacted. Even though these are all a part of a historic beginning, many of these have been more sporadic than systematic. They have accomplished much and given great encouragement to the body of Christ, but these are just the forerunners of what is to come. In modern military terms, these have been like the Special Forces that have been dropped behind enemy lines before the main assault is to begin. It is now time for the main assault.

As I wrote in 1987, a spiritual advance was going to come that would be so great that many would consider it the harvest that is the end of the age. However, it was not the final harvest, but simply the reaping and the preparing of those who would be the laborers for the harvest that truly would be the end of this age. A great wave came to whole continents shortly after I wrote that, and it was so great that many thought it was the last harvest, but as I saw then, there is another greater one coming. It may be beginning to break as I write this, because a mighty outpouring of the Spirit has begun in just the last few months. If this is it, we will see it eclipse all other previous waves of the Spirit.

The Battle Begins

When the Israelites crossed the Jordan River, the first thing they faced was possibly the most powerful and most fortified stronghold of all. Jericho seemed impregnable to the entire known world at the time. How would the Israelites, who had never even had a land of their own, conquer Jericho? In every way it was impossible for them, but everything since their departure from Egypt had been impossible too. They were used to doing the impossible. They knew that they were dependent on God for the victory, that they had to have a miracle, and so do we. What is coming is beyond human ingenuity to accomplish.

Even with the great multitude that the church has now become, what we are facing is still much bigger, much stronger, and a much more strongly entrenched enemy than what we can overcome with either our numbers or our wisdom. We are facing supernatural strongholds that have had millenniums to sink their roots deeper and deeper into the hearts of men. This is a spiritual battle that is going to take a remarkable unity and obedience of God's people just as it did when Israel faced Jericho. It is going to take the supernatural power of God to prevail. It will therefore take great faith in Him to proceed. That is the point. It is not weapons or strategies that we need as much as faith in God.

The crossing of the Jordan River when it was over-flowing all of its banks was meant to begin unifying the tribes of Israel in a much greater way than they had ever known before. Their advance began with a great supernatural demonstration from God. They could not have even made it into the land without the Lord. However, He required that they step into the water before He performed the miracle. By His directions, our part is to step forward into the impossible circumstances.

Many want to see miracles, but few want to be put into the circumstances where they will have to have one. Just getting to the land will take a miracle, and then bringing down the very first stronghold will take an even bigger one! The beginning of the battle is rarely against the external enemy, but instead it is the one we have to fight within just to move toward the battle. The biggest battle will be to not put our attention on how difficult the circumstances are, how strong the enemy is, or how weak we are, but how great God is. As long as we can do this, the victory is sure.

CROSSING OVER 8

The world is facing earthquakes, tsunamis, storms, and plagues such as AIDS, and those threatening such as the bird flu, not to mention the seemingly inevitable human conflicts that are looming. It does look as if we are entering a period when the spiritual Jordan River will be overflowing all of its banks. In terms of loss of human life, recent natural disasters have already been the worst in human history. Again, this is like the spiritual conditions prophesied, with the strategy of what we should do, as we read in Joshua 3:3-4, 14-17:

> "When you see the ark of the covenant of the LORD your God with the Levitical priests carrying it, then you shall set out from your place and go after it.

> "However, there shall be between you and it a distance of about 2,000 cubits by measure. Do not come near it, that you may know the way by which you shall go, for you have not passed this way before."

So it came about when the people set out from their tents to cross the Jordan with the priests carrying the ark of the covenant before the people,

and when those who carried the ark came into the Jordan, and the feet of the priests carrying the ark were dipped in the edge of the water (for the Jordan overflows all its banks all the days of harvest),

that the waters which were flowing down from above stood and rose up in one heap, a great distance away at Adam, the city that is beside Zarethan; and those which were flowing down toward the sea of the Arabah, the Salt Sea, were completely cut off. So the people crossed opposite Jericho.

And the priests who carried the ark of the covenant of the Lord stood firm on dry ground in the middle of the Jordan while all Israel crossed on dry ground, until all the nation had finished crossing the Jordan.

As discussed, the reason why the Lord commanded the Ark to be carried across the Jordan **"about"** 2,000 cubits ahead of the rest of the people was that the Ark represents Jesus, and the cubits represent years. This was a prophetic statement that the Lord would pass through death to His Promised Land "about" 2,000 years before the rest of His people. It is now "about" 2,000 years, and the time has come. When natural and human disasters come, it is not time to draw back, to hide and to horde, but it is time to cross over. It is the time of the greatest harvest that has ever been reaped. Life will prevail over death. The kingdom is at hand. This is not a sign of the end of the world, but a new beginning. This age is ending, and the new one, in which Christ Jesus will take His authority over the earth and reign, is about to begin.

At the same time that such great troubles are coming upon the world, those who are walking in the ways of the Lord are going to prosper more than they ever have before, which means their lives will also be overflowing all of their previous banks or limits. We see this stated as the condition that should be normal for every Christian in II Corinthians 9:8:

> **And God is able to make all grace abound to you, that always having all sufficiency in everything, you may have an abundance for every good deed.**

If we are living in our inheritance, which are all of the benefits of our citizenship in heaven, we should be walking in **"all grace,"** not just some, having **"all sufficiency in everything,"** not just some things, and have **"an abundance for every good deed,"** not just some abundance for some good deeds. That is the state of the normal Christian life that has possessed the inheritance.

We should note that in the preceding verses this is the result of generous sowing, which is also normal Christianity. We should sow seed, expecting a harvest, not just so we can increase our standard of living, but our standard of giving. The spiritually mature will have a contentment about material things and a moderation in all things. The mature Christian will never be as focused on the stuff in this life as much as laying up treasure for eternal life. Even so, how we handle money is very important. The Lord said that we could not be trusted with the "true treasures" if we do not learn how to handle **"unrighteous mammon"** (**see Luke 16:11**) properly.

The Greatest Hope

In Joshua 3:16, we are told that the waters of the Jordan **"which were flowing down from above stood and rose up in one heap, a great distance away at Adam."** It was no accident that this little town was named **"Adam,"** just as there are no accidents at all in Scripture. This was a prophecy that when God's people began to pass through this baptism in the Jordan, entering into this life that truly takes up the cross every day, dying to ourselves so that we can be alive to Him, death will be rolled back all the way to Adam! All of the death that was the consequence of the Fall will be turned back.

When God's people possess their inheritance, it will begin the **"period of the restoration of all things"** (**see Acts 3:21**). Peter spoke about, which is stated often by the prophets, the time when the earth will be restored to the paradise it was originally intended to be. The lions will lie down with the lambs, children will play with cobras, all sickness and disease will be done away with, no one will hurt anyone else, and there will not be any more tears—all of this is *on the earth*.

The ultimate revelation of God's nature will forever be the history of earth. When mankind rebelled against Him, He did not destroy us, but He came and lived among us, and then laid down His own life for our redemption. One of the most awesome demonstrations of God's character will be how He did not leave the earth in its depravity, but He restored it all the way back from where it had fallen.

No utopian philosophy and no other religion have been given such a great hope for the earth and for mankind as has been given to us. We must not allow the cults and false religions to keep stealing the high ground of hope for the future when we have been given the greatest hope of all. That hope is the gospel of the kingdom that is coming—the gospel that must be preached throughout the world before the end can come. It is the end of the age, but not the end of the world—a new beginning. This is good news! In the times to come, this great hope will be even brighter against the darkness, and it will turn many toward the highway that is being built in preparation for it.

So as Israel crossed over in type and had to destroy or drive the inhabitants out, we are crossing over with this most powerful weapon, the greatest message of hope the world has ever heard—to possess the nations as an inheritance for Christ and to set them free from their bondage. This will take place when the very fabric of the society, built by fallen human nature, will be coming apart. The earth itself will also be groaning and travailing, causing great natural disasters. This will all make the gospel of the coming kingdom even more brilliant. The nations will come to the light of this gospel. We are entering the times that even the prophets of old desired to see.

Victory Over Death

Our goal is to see death defeated. We are victorious over death by laying down our lives for Christ. Baptism is a ritual performed to emphasize an important spiritual reality. One of the most tragic mistakes of Christianity since the third century has been to try to substitute rituals for the realities that they represented. The ritual of baptism was intended to be a commitment to lay down our own lives in order to live for Christ. After the third century, one could be baptized in place of living the crucified life, removing the life and power of the cross from the church.

We do not want to belittle the importance of the ritual. A wedding is a ritual, and not the marriage itself, but because marriage is so important it is right to make a big deal out of the ritual of marriage. Likewise, it is right to make a big deal out of baptism, communion, and the other important rituals handed down to us, but they must not be allowed to supplant the truths that they were given to illuminate. You can dunk someone in the water all day and not have them partake of the death or resurrection of Jesus. Nothing is magical about the water. The power is in the crucified life. The baptism is performed as a commitment to live the crucified life in order that we might also be resurrected with Christ as we read in Romans 6:4:

> **Therefore we have been buried with Him through baptism into death, in order that as Christ was raised from the dead through the glory of the Father, so we too might walk in newness of life.**

Note that in this text there is no mention of water! This is not speaking of water baptism, but of what water baptism represents—the crucified life. As Paul further conveyed in Romans 6:5: **"For if we have become united with Him in the likeness of His death, certainly we shall also be in the likeness of His resurrection."** That is the true baptism.

This is what the Lord meant when He said, **"I have come to cast fire upon the earth; and how I wish it were already kindled! But I have a baptism to undergo, and how distressed I am until it is accomplished!"** (Luke 12:49-50) Was the baptism that was distressing Him simply being immersed in water? Of course not. He was referring to His impending crucifixion. That crucifixion is also the meaning of our baptism. We are baptized into Christ by embracing the cross.

Jesus was likewise referring to the baptism into His crucifixion when James and John asked to be seated on His right and left in the kingdom. **"But Jesus said to them, 'You do not know what you are asking for. Are you able to drink the cup that I drink, or to be baptized with the baptism with which I am baptized?'"** (Mark 10:38)

Again, it is a basic spiritual principle that death is the path to life in Christ. We are called to live our present lives by the power and authority of the resurrected life of Christ. By its very definition one cannot experience a resurrection without first experiencing a death. To be baptized with His baptism is to be conformed to the purpose of His death, the laying down of our own lives for the sake of others.

When the church reduced the truth of the crucified life to a mere ritual it robbed the Lord of His people's consecration, it robbed the church of its salvation, and it robbed the world of the power of the gospel. Many Scriptures corroborate this truth. The following are just a few of them:

For if we died with Him, we shall also live with Him;

if we endure, we shall also reign with Him (see II Timothy 2:11-12).

The Spirit Himself bears witness with our spirit that we are the children of God,

and if children, heirs also, heirs of God and fellow heirs with Christ, IF INDEED WE SUFFER WITH HIM *IN ORDER THAT* we may also be glorified with Him (Romans 8:16-17).

That I may know Him, and the power of His resurrection and the FELLOWSHIP OF HIS SUFFERINGS, being conformed to His death;

IN ORDER THAT I may attain to the resurrection from the dead (Philippians 3:10-11).

For to you it has been granted for Christ's sake, not only to believe in Him, but also to suffer for His sake (Philippians 1:29).

We ought always to give thanks to God for you, brethren, as is only fitting, because your faith is greatly enlarged, and the love of each one of you toward one another grows ever greater;

therefore, we ourselves speak proudly of you among the churches of God for your perseverance and faith in the midst of all your persecutions and afflictions which you endure.

This is a plain indication of God's righteous judgment so that you may be considered worthy of the kingdom of God, for which indeed you are suffering (II Thessalonians 1:3-5).

We are afflicted in every way, but not crushed; perplexed, but not despairing;

persecuted, but not forsaken; struck down, but not destroyed;

ALWAYS carrying about in the body the dying of Jesus, that the life of Jesus also may be manifested in our body.

For we who live are constantly being delivered over to death for Jesus' sake, that the life of Jesus also may be manifested in our mortal flesh (II Corinthians 4:8-11).

In the first century, some of the people thought that if they would circumcise their flesh they would be right with God, but as the New Testament explains, the Lord requires the circumcision of our hearts. Some today point to the day of their immersion as the day they died with Jesus and were resurrected. That was the day of their commitment, but it does not fulfill the commitment any more than a wedding is a marriage. Every ritual is just that—a ritual that is meant to symbolize a commitment to the spiritual reality of which it speaks. In Christ, we must die in order to live. The Lord Jesus made this clear:

> **"If anyone wishes to come after Me, let him deny himself, and take up his cross, and follow Me.**
>
> **"For whoever wishes to save his life shall lose it; but whoever loses his life for My sake shall find it" (see Matthew 16:24-25).**

There can be no question that the Lord intended our baptism to be the daily reality of a crucified life. However, as we have already discussed, such a life that dies to itself and its own selfish interests is the most free and powerful life of all. That is what the Lord will give to us in exchange for our life—the greatest freedom and the greatest power to do good that we could even know. This is the gate to possessing all the promises of God. To lay down our own lives to do His will is the greatest opportunity and the greatest transaction that one could ever make.

THE BAPTISM OF LIFE

As the church is now drawing up to its spiritual Jordan River and preparing to cross over, we can expect the cross to become an emphasis again, and the crucified life to be a hallmark of all who follow the Lord. That is basic to the church being mature enough to inherit her Promised Land, which in Christ are the nations.

Here I am emphasizing the corporate truths of the Jordan River, but these principles apply to us as individuals as well. In a sense, we go through this process with every inheritance of a promise of God. The principle is true that between the place where we receive the promise and the fulfillment of that promise there will almost always be a wilderness that is the exact opposite of what we have been promised. This is where our faith in God grows and our character is transformed so that we can handle our inheritance.

When Israel entered into this baptism in the Red Sea, it resulted in the destruction of her enemies which had kept them in bondage for so long. Pharaoh and his army were a biblical type of Satan and his hordes which seek to keep God's people in bondage, but we see that baptism is the one place where they could not follow. When God's people enter into the true baptism, it will result in the destruction of the evil that has been keeping us in bondage. When Israel entered into that baptism, they were to never see those enemies again, and many of the things that have bound us for so long will likewise be destroyed when we enter this baptism.

The Jordan River represents a second baptism, but it is also the same as the Red Sea. It is a second devotion to live the life of the cross. Deuteronomy means "a second law," and the Book of Deuteronomy was the result of Moses reviewing everything for Israel that was required of them before they crossed over to possess their land. Likewise, there is a baptism that we go through when we first begin to follow the Lord, and a second commitment to this that is usually required before we enter our Promised Land.

Like Israel, we often forget many of the basics after years of walking with the Lord. However, the most successful people in any field are those who do the basics best, and the greatest Christians are those who do the basics best. Therefore, we can expect a period of time in which an extraordinary anointing will come upon the teaching of the basics of the faith, especially the crucified life. This is not taking us back to spiritual infancy, but the necessary fortifying of the basics so we can win the battles that are ahead of us. Many have drifted away from their former commitments to the crucified life during their wilderness years. That we are being drawn back to the cross in these times is a sign that we are about to cross over and start possessing all that we have been called to. This is grace from God.

When we leave Egypt there is a baptism, and when we enter the Promised Land there is a baptism. This is a message that the cross is both the beginning and the end of our journey. The cross both sets us free from the world (Egypt), and is the door to entering into our inheritance in Christ.

I have now spent nearly forty years studying church history, and I have come to see how one of the greatest messages of this history is how those who accomplished great things lived the life of the cross. The message of the cross is sown throughout their messages. The testimony of their contemporaries was that they lived it as well. However, it is rare to hear the message of the cross, or the call to the crucified life in messages today, or in modern Christian works. We can expect this to change.

It is understood that we do not want to stay at the cross but proceed to the resurrection, yet neither can we bypass the cross. The cross is the only path to the resurrected life. Many have tried to live in the power of the resurrected life of Christ without taking up their crosses daily. This inevitably results in self-centeredness—an overwhelming emphasis on ourselves instead of Christ. The wise and mature are forever mindful that the cross is everything. However, the cross does not just represent death but the door to resurrection life, which is also represented by the Promised Land.

The Great Change

I was told by the Spirit more than two decades ago that the cross would be popular again, and it would be the time when the church enters into her finest hour. We are now at that time. Before proceeding let's go back for just a moment to look at another major difference between the two baptisms—the first represented by the Red Sea and the other is represented by the Jordan River. A major difference between these is that the Israelites did not go to the Red Sea baptism willingly, but this will be different when they enter the Jordan. At the Red Sea, the Lord had to basically trick them into it as we read in Exodus 13:17-18 and 14:1-4.

> Now it came about when Pharaoh had let the people go, that God did not lead them by the way of the land of the Philistines, even though it was near; for God said, "Lest the people change their minds when they see war, and they return to Egypt."
>
> Hence God led the people around by the way of the wilderness to the Red Sea....
>
> Now the LORD spoke to Moses, saying, "Tell the sons of Israel to turn back and camp before Pi-hahiroth, between Migdol and the sea...."

"For Pharaoh will say of the sons of Israel,
'They are wandering aimlessly in the land;
the wilderness has shut them in.'

"Thus I will harden Pharaoh's heart, and he
will chase after them; and I will be honored
through Pharaoh and all his army, and the
Egyptians will know that I am the LORD."
And they did so.

The only way that the Lord could get Israel to partake
of the Red Sea baptism was to corner them into it. As
we look back on most of the trials that have been used
to fashion our lives, we will probably have to confess
the same thing—we did not choose the trials. We were
cornered into them the same way. We must remember
what He has promised us in I Corinthians 10:13:

No temptation has overtaken you but such
as is common to man; and God is faithful,
who will not allow you to be tempted beyond
what you are able, but with the temptation
will provide the way of escape also, that you
may be able to endure it.

We can be sure that He never allows us to go through
anything we cannot handle. We also can be sure He
will always give us a way of escape. That way of escape
is the same way—to die! In every trial we do not have
to go to the cross—we get to! It is the path to life. It is
the grace of the Lord to align our circumstances that
there is absolutely no way out but to lay down our
lives and conform to the image of His death.

During this time the Lord also usually fixes it so that the enemy is chasing us. To retreat only means that we end up at the end of his spears. This is when we learn that the two most powerful beings in the universe are both trying to kill us! One of them is going to get the job done, and we must choose which one it will be. That, too, is actually grace from the Lord.

However, it will be different with the Jordan River baptism. The more mature Christians who have made it through the wilderness have grown in faith and do not have to be tricked or trapped into their baptism any longer—they willingly choose to take up their crosses. The mature do not run from the cross but to it.

The Prevailing Heart

The church, as a whole, is no longer just recently released slaves—we are warriors with the greatest cause, preparing for the greatest battle. Yet probably ten negative comments are heard about the church today for every encouraging one. However, complaints are mostly coming from those who do not have eyes to see or are still wandering in circles in the wilderness.

Think about the following facts. In 1960, it was estimated that 30 million people had been empowered by the baptism in the Holy Spirit. Today, there are over twenty times that many and we are approaching one billion! Many of the greatest pastors, teachers, and evangelists in the history of the church are alive today. An emerging prophetic ministry is rising to the true biblical standards of that calling with the kind of prophetic gifts that are beginning to rival anything seen in the Old Testament and will undoubtedly exceed them. A new breed of ministry is arising that will walk in true apostolic stature, authority, and wisdom.

After every great move of God, there was a lull before the next one. However, each new move of God would exceed the limits of the previous one by a considerable margin. The much maligned Charismatic movement actually resulted in more salvations, more churches being planted, more missions being birthed, and more missionaries being sent out, than possibly all of the previous moves of God combined. Yet, it is almost always discussed in a negative light even by Christian leaders. We should want every failure to be that successful!

Though there have been a number of great movements arise since the Charismatic movement peaked, they have been tiny in comparison, so there has been a seeming lull since the peak of that movement, at least in the West. However, we can expect the move of God that is now building to eclipse even the Charismatic movement in breadth as well as depth. The one that is now building is truly going to be something to behold. As I write this, we have had months of such a remarkable outpouring of the Spirit in our home church. We estimate that we have seen more and greater miracles during the past twenty weeks than in the previous twenty years, and we have seen a lot over the years. Obviously, we are in the first stages of a new move of

God that is starting off more powerful than the last one ended in many ways. This is the beginning of what the prophets and righteous men of old all desired to see and have been waiting for as members of the great cloud of witnesses.

It is wonderful to see this unfolding, but how do we, personally, become a part of this? I was shown what it will take when I was asked to speak to a few National Football League teams before their games. The intensity of the focus on their faces was like nothing I had seen since being in the military. When I was speaking to the Denver Broncos before an important Monday night game with their rivals, the Kansas City Chiefs, the Lord drew my attention to their "game faces." Then He said to me, "When you see that kind of focus on My people, the time is at hand."

Since that night I have looked for the increasing focus on the faces of God's people everywhere I go. For years, it seemed that in most churches the people were more like kids in detention after school than in a rising, conquering army. In the last few years, this has been changing, and I have begun to see the increasing focus, the intensity, which I know means that the great advance is now close. In the last few months, it has reached an electrifying peak.

When speaking to those football teams just before a game, I did at times think that if they were not released on their foe very soon they would begin to hurt each other! That is what has happened in many churches. When we build people up and then do not release

108

them on the enemy, in their frustration they can turn on each other. This is the cause of many church splits and other problems. It is now time for us to engage the enemy. We need church builders, and this is a job that some will always need to be occupied with, but it is now time to turn our attention away from just building up ourselves to building the kingdom. We must have a jailbreak and break out of the prison walls of our churches.

Again, this is not to imply that the work on us is finished, but much of the deep inner workings that we need now can only come from the battles we are called to fight with the enemy. The worst enemy of Christianity is complacency, or as the Lord put it, *lukewarmness*. This is the greatest delusion and deception of all. How could anyone truly know the Lord, the Consuming Fire, and not be on fire for Him and His gospel? That is why His true messengers are "flames of fire."

Lukewarmness is not possible without the delusions of the cares and worries of this world having choked out the seed of His word in us. This is often because believers get bored or frustrated with their church life, and turn back to the world for satisfaction or fulfillment. They may still go to services, read their Bibles, pray, and go through the other motions of being a Christian, but their affections are turned more and more to the things of the world. This may be the state of most Christians in the West at this time. However, there is nothing that can shake someone out of complacency like war. If there is ever a greater focus than you will see on a professional football team before a game, it will be on the faces of soldiers before a battle. When the church becomes the army that she is called to be, and begins engaging in the battles she is called to fight, a great change will come upon the church.

Even King David, one of the greatest souls to ever walk the earth and one of the greatest pursuers of God of all time, stayed at home during the time "when kings go out to battle." He fell into adultery and opened the door for some of the worst problems of his life. When it is time to fight and we do not fight, we are almost certain to be overcome and defeated by the enemy in some way. Now is the time when we must go on the offensive and start looking to missions that do not just selfishly build our own church, but begin to take territory for the kingdom of God. Our churches would then grow and become much stronger than they are.

We were created with a need for adventure. No greater adventure happens in this life than the true Christian life. Youth especially need adventure in their lives, and the emerging generation will not endure sitting in boring church services. If they are not captured by missions in some form, they are very likely to be captured by the spirit of the world.

Probably nothing is more boring than religion. C.S. Lewis once said his definition of hell was to sit in an endless church service without the presence of God. Such services are from hell, and one of the great devices of the devil is to capture and imprison believers in a boring form of religion that has no power. Again, we need a jailbreak, and then we need to take up our divinely powerful weapons and start to engage the enemy, taking the land that is rightfully ours.

Any church that is not actively engaged in missions will whither away, if not physically, at least spiritually. However, we do not just want to be engaged in missions but in *our* mission. We need to be sent out by the Lord and led by Him. We need specific goals for our missions so we can measure the progress, success, or failure of them. We need to define the Promised Land that we are crossing over to conquer. Even before crossing the Jordan, the Promised Land was divided up between the tribes of Israel. They were all to fight together and to keep fighting until all of the tribes had possessed their land. We need to do the same. Certain spiritual tribes, denominations, or movements need to define the territory they are to take, and we need to help each other do it.

Over the last few years, there have been gatherings of some of the great leaders of our time from many different movements. From these gatherings, other councils have been forming and divine strategies illuminated. They are still very much in their formative stages, but there is a remarkable anointing on them. There is no question that an unprecedented advance of the gospel is at hand. It may yet be a few years unfolding in all of its power, but it is at hand. Therefore, we can expect the vision of our Promised Land to become more clear, and the strategies for taking it more specific.

THE HEART OF A FIGHTER 10

As we have been covering, the church now stands on the brink of one of the most important advances in history, which must now take place. For the church to continue wandering in the wilderness, it would only wither away. We are called to be sojourners but not nomads. Sojourners are traveling to a destination while nomads just wander. We are coming to the destination that the entire church age has been preparing us for and now must go forward.

The conquest of the Promised Land was a combination of the people fighting and the Lord fighting for them. He wanted them to be involved, and they had to have Him involved. It was a partnership, which is the case with every move of God. Those who want God to do everything never accomplish anything, and those who try to do everything themselves will fail. It takes knowledge of the Lord's ways, wisdom, and understanding to walk the fine line to be yoked with the

Lord and doing His work. However, the real strength, wisdom, and power for it is coming from Him.

To take a yoke speaks of work, but if a tiny little ox is yoked with a big one, who is going to be doing the real work? That is how we are yoked with Him. Without question, this is Him doing the work, and He lets us come along to be a part of it, but it is still a partnership. He will not do the work without us being yoked to Him so that He can work through us. We are His body on the earth now.

It takes spiritual wisdom and maturity to walk in this narrow way, the balance between doing our own works and being joined to Him in His work. Just as Israel at times drifted from this fine line and was defeated before their enemies when they did, we are already too foolish and immature if we think we are so wise as not to make some of the same mistakes. However, like Israel we must resolve to learn from every mistake, draw close to the Lord again, and keep pressing ahead. We cannot keep letting our mistakes stop us like they have in so many previous revivals, awakenings, renewals, and advances in the past.

If we are going to succeed, one of the first things we must leave behind is the idealism that is rooted in humanism that would make us think everything will go smoothly and without problems. We can expect the Lord's leadership to be perfect, but we can also expect our following Him to lapse at times. The combination of the divine and the human makes for a continually interesting and sometimes frustrating experience. However, the

Lord knew we were not perfect when He called us, and He already knew all the mistakes we would make, and He still called us! Even so, the more closely we follow Him, the easier and faster it will go.

After crossing, several prophetic events were required that intended to seal their unity and commitment to obedience. We, too, must learn these before going further.

First, Joshua was commanded to have the priests take twelve stones from the middle of the Jordan River and build a monument that would continually remind all of Israel of their crossing of the Jordan, as we read in Joshua 4:19-24:

> **Now the people came up from the Jordan on the tenth of the first month and camped at Gilgal on the eastern edge of Jericho.**
>
> **And those twelve stones which they had taken from the Jordan, Joshua set them up at Gilgal.**
>
> **And he then said to the sons of Israel, "When your children ask their fathers in time to come, saying, 'What are these stones?'**
>
> **"Then you shall inform your children, saying, 'Israel crossed this Jordan on dry ground.'**
>
> **"For the LORD your God dried up the waters of the Jordan before you until you had crossed, just as the LORD your God had done to the Red Sea, which He dried up before us until we had crossed;**

**"that all the peoples of the earth may know
that the hand of the LORD is mighty, so that
you may fear the LORD your God forever."**

This was a crucial deed for Israel. First, it would
forever remind them that it was not their wisdom or
strength that had enabled them to cross the Jordan. It
was the Lord, by His strength, that had enabled them
to cross over **"on dry ground,"** even while the river of
death was overflowing all of its banks. Such monuments
are important for the generations to come who did
not personally witness the things that their forbearers
experienced with God.

Many movements did not have the wisdom to build
monuments to what the Lord had done for them, and
they withered away after a generation or two. Others
came to trouble because they stayed at the monument
and began to worship it. A ditch is on either side of the
path of life that we can fall into. Even so, the building
of a monument for the right reason is not only the
right thing to do, but an important thing to do. It is
righteous to always be thinking of the generations to
come—to build bridges to them that will keep leading
them to the Lord.

The second reason why this was important was that it
reminded all of Israel that the twelve stones represented
twelve tribes. Regardless of which tribe they were a
part of, they were all a part of one nation. Just as the
high priest had to wear the stones of all of the tribes
on his breastplate or on his heart, if we are going to
walk in the high calling of God, we must keep all of
God's people on our hearts, not just our tribe.

The Whole Is Greater Than the Sum of Its Parts

Each tribe was special and had its own calling and own inheritance, but they also had to keep their vision and understanding of how they fit into the whole nation of Israel—its vision and purpose. The body of Christ also needs the constant reminder that even though we may be a part of a certain movement or denomination, which has its own calling and inheritance, we are all members of one body, the "Holy Nation."

Before Joshua let the priests leave the Jordan, he made sure that this monument was built. Unity is not something that just happens—it needs to be worked at. Make it an issue; focus on it; and keep teaching it. Such monuments can help this as long as they do not become a stopping point.

One thing that we started doing the first year we planted our church in Charlotte was to close down all meetings and services for the month of July and encourage the members of our church to visit other churches in the city. This helped to give them a vision for what God was doing in His whole body, not just our little part. We also tell them that if they find a place where they fit better than with us, they are free to stay, letting the Holy Spirit place them in the body where it pleases Him.

Of course, the first week of August we do not have any idea who will be coming back, but to date there have always been more on the first week of August than we had at the end of June. Some do leave and find a place that they fit better with than with us, and we are happy about it. We may miss them, but we feel that this is helping to build the whole body, and that by sending them out this way we can have fruit that grows in other fields. We have also learned that if a member is supposed to be in another congregation, they will become trouble if they stay with us because they will not fit.

We want to walk in the highest purposes of God that we can, and to do this, we must, like the high priest, keep all of the tribes, all of God's people, on our hearts. The unity of His people was the main thing that the Lord prayed about the last night that He was on this earth as a man. If you knew that tonight was your last night on this earth, do you think your prayers would be focused on what are truly the deepest matters of your heart? I think the prayer the Lord prayed that night reveals the heart of God more than any other teaching that He gave. If we are going to be in unity with Him, we will have this same heart for the unity of His people.

Any part of the body that grows without regard to the rest of the body is a cancer. We do not want to be a cancer, but a blessing to the whole body. What we do each July has now become something of a testament. It has been an astonishing thing to many other pastors, causing some to want to get to know us better. It has been intimidating and threatening to those who are overly possessive and controlling with their people, causing them to make harsh accusations about us. We cannot help that. We are doing what we do out of obedience, and it is unquestionably doing good for us and for others. We have been able to help a number of other congregations grow by sending them some very good people.

This is not for every congregation to do, and we hold it as a principle for us not a law. We have already determined that when revival breaks out we may not be able to stop and take a month off like this. For the first time in our history, the breakout that we experienced this year caused us not to shut the meetings down in July. What was happening could not be stopped. True revival is like the labor of a woman giving birth, and regardless of whether it is the Sabbath or any other holiday, we cannot just decide to stop labor and take a vacation. However, this practice has been very healthy for us. One other church that heard about this and tried it said that it was one of the best things they ever did for their congregation. Even so, I do not recommend doing this just because it is working for us, but follow the Lord in what He is calling you to do.

We really are all one body in Christ, and those who go to another part where they fit better help to bring us closer to the whole body. If people are sent out on good terms, they usually stay on good terms, often coming to visit, attending our conferences, or other special meetings. They also usually bring others from their new home congregation and their leadership often come, not being intimidated by the possibility of us "taking their people" because we have already proven we are not trying to do that.

119

The Holy Spirit is going to be where there is liberty, as we read in II Corinthians 3:17. Also, the Lord made a remarkable promise for those who come into unity, as we read in Matthew 18:19-20:

> **"Again I say to you, that if two of you agree on earth about anything that they may ask, it shall be done for them by My Father who is in heaven.**

> **"For where two or three have gathered together in My name, there I am in their midst."**

The Greek word that is translated **"agree"** here is *sumphoneo,* which literally means "to be harmonious" or "in one accord." It is more than just assenting that the prayer is for the right thing, but it is speaking of a deep and true unity. The power of unity is that if just two of us have it, we can ask "anything" and the Father will do it. He can trust those who are in unity with that kind of power because for them to come to such a place they have obviously obtained a high degree of spiritual maturity and humility. This will be the kind of power that we are going to need for the battles ahead, so pursuing unity must be a high priority. That is why it is important for us to take the time to build whatever monuments that will continually remind us of our unity and common destiny.

This chapter is titled "The Heart of a Fighter" because what we are discussing here is fundamental to the heart of a fighter. True freedom fighters in the Spirit do not fight because they are angry or greedy for something others possess, but because they love. It is because of our love for the Lord that we resolve to die rather than compromise His truth. It is because of our love for one another that we will fight for the inheritance of the whole body, not just our own inheritance. That is how Israel fought for their inheritance—all of the tribes kept fighting as one until all of God's people had possessed their inheritance.

As Mike Bickle, the director of the International House of Prayer in Kansas City, once pointed out, "Anyone will quit except a person in love." This is an important truth. Love is the heart of the fighters who overcome, attaining their own inheritance, as well as those of all of God's people, because our inheritance is linked to everyone else's. Selfishness and self-centeredness have no place in the kingdom of God. The heart of the true freedom fighter is love and the devotion to unity.

DELIVERANCE FROM DEATH

The next prophetic event that Israel experienced was also at Gilgal. After Joshua had set up the monument of the twelve stones, he was then instructed by the Lord to make flint knives and circumcise all of the males who had been born in the wilderness because they had not yet been circumcised. Since circumcision represents the removal of the flesh or the carnal nature, this had to be done before Israel could go into battle for their inheritance.

Likewise today, many Christians have walked with the Lord for a long time, and experienced many things with Him along the way, yet they are still carrying their carnal nature, but it can go no further. We cannot possess our inheritance while still living according to our carnal nature, as we are told very clearly in Galatians 5:13-21:

> **For you were called to freedom, brethren;**
> **only *do* not *turn* your freedom into an**

opportunity for the flesh, but through love serve one another.

For the whole Law is fulfilled in one word, in the *statement*, "You shall love your neighbor as yourself."

But if you bite and devour one another, take care lest you be consumed by one another.

But I say, walk by the Spirit, and you will not carry out the desire of the flesh.

For the flesh sets its desire against the Spirit, and the Spirit against the flesh; for these are in opposition to one another, so that you may not do the things that you please.

But if you are led by the Spirit, you are not under the Law.

Now the deeds of the flesh are evident, which are: immorality, impurity, sensuality,

idolatry, sorcery, enmities, strife, jealousy, outbursts of anger, disputes, dissensions, factions,

envying, drunkenness, carousing, and things like these, of which I forewarn you just as I have forewarned you that those who practice such things will not inherit the kingdom of God.

The apostle makes clear, **"those who practice such things will not inherit the kingdom of God."** We will not be able to enter into our inheritance while still living by this carnal nature, and it must be cut away.

Like the other rituals, circumcision was intended as a commitment to circumcise our hearts. The reason why it was commanded in the Law to be performed on the eighth day after one was born is because eight is the number of new beginnings. The way our heart is circumcised is by being born again—partaking of the new life we have been given in Christ in exchange for our old life.

Obviously, when we are born again we do not become instantly perfect, and it seems to just begin the great battle with our old, carnal nature. It is a process which requires the renewing of our minds, which is kind of like getting rid of the gofers. The gofer holes are still there, the habit patterns, and the entanglements that can keep pulling us back into the carnal nature—however, when we are born again and receive the renewing, regenerating power of the Holy Spirit into our lives, we are empowered to overcome sin and our sinful nature.

Sin does not have to have dominion over us anymore, but as James wrote, we do still all **"stumble in many ways" (see James 3:2).** Even so, for those who are true disciples and followers of Christ, they fight to put down this nature and walk in newness of life.

So how do we get free? **"And in Him you were also circumcised with a circumcision made without hands, in the removal of the body of the flesh by the circumcision of Christ" (Colossians 2:11).**

The New Testament is filled with wisdom and encouragement about how to do this, but the Book of Romans is especially helpful. Maybe this is why when so many

125

of the great saints in history were asked if they could only have one book of the Bible which would it be, many replied that it would be the Book of Romans. This Book not only contains the most comprehensive teaching on New Covenant theology, but it also includes some of the most basic and practical wisdom about how to live the New Covenant life.

For this reason, I am going to quote from the Book of Romans quite extensively in this chapter; the wise will not just cruise over it, but carefully and prayerfully consider its teaching. Scripture itself will always be much more powerful than any commentary we can give on it, and the wise always give more heed to Scripture quotations than to the commentary. I am also doing this because Paul articulated these principles that are so important about as well as they can be stated. We begin with Romans 6:

> **What shall we say then? Are we to continue in sin that grace might increase?**
>
> **May it never be! How shall we who died to sin still live in it?**
>
> **Or do you not know that all of us who have been baptized into Christ Jesus have been baptized into His death?**
>
> **Therefore we have been buried with Him through baptism into death, in order that as Christ was raised from the dead through the glory of the Father, so we too might walk in newness of life.**

For if we have become united with *Him* in the likeness of His death, certainly we shall be also *in the likeness* of His resurrection,

knowing this, that our old self was crucified with *Him*, that our body of sin might be done away with, that we should no longer be slaves to sin;

for he who has died is freed from sin.

Now if we have died with Christ, we believe that we shall also live with Him,

knowing that Christ, having been raised from the dead, is never to die again; death no longer is master over Him.

For the death that He died, He died to sin, once for all; but the life that He lives, He lives to God.

Even so consider yourselves to be dead to sin, but alive to God in Christ Jesus.

Therefore do not let sin reign in your mortal body that you should obey its lusts,

and do not go on presenting the members of your body to sin *as* instruments of unrighteousness; but present yourselves to God as those alive from the dead, and your members *as* instruments of righteousness to God.

For sin shall not be master over you, for you are not under law, but under grace.

What then? Shall we sin because we are not under law but under grace? May it never be!

Do you not know that when you present yourselves to someone *as* slaves for obedience, you are slaves of the one whom you obey, either of sin resulting in death, or of obedience resulting in righteousness?

But thanks be to God that though you were slaves of sin, you became obedient from the heart to that form of teaching to which you were committed,

and having been freed from sin, you became slaves of righteousness.

I am speaking in human terms because of the weakness of your flesh. For just as you presented your members *as* slaves to impurity and to lawlessness, resulting in *further* lawlessness, so now present your members *as* slaves to righteousness, resulting in sanctification.

For when you were slaves of sin, you were free in regard to righteousness.

Therefore what benefit were you then deriving from the things of which you are now ashamed? For the outcome of those things is death.

But now having been freed from sin and enslaved to God, you derive your benefit, resulting in sanctification, and the outcome, eternal life.

For the wages of sin is death, but the free gift of God is eternal life in Christ Jesus our Lord (Romans 6:1-23).

If this text makes us feel uncomfortable or convicted, that is what it is meant to do. There is a difference between conviction and condemnation. Conviction is meant to lead to our repentance and deliverance from the sin that has entangled us so that we will not be condemned.

What the Scripture calls a **"doctrine of demons," (see I Timothy 4:1)** preaches forgiveness without repentance which is more than just feeling sorry about the sin, but true repentance is to turn away from the sin. It is a doctrine of demons that also tries to change or rationalize the clear Word of God and say that what God has called sin is not a sin. It is the grace of God that has sent the Holy Spirit to convict us of our sin, and then point us to the cross of Jesus, the only remedy for sin. At the cross, we are not only forgiven but we are also changed and given a new life in place of the sin nature that has been killing us.

The flint knife of the spiritual circumcision is supposed to hurt. Conviction hurts, but it hurts good, and it will lead to our salvation. Again, it is a false gospel that asserts that the grace of God is the perpetual forgiveness of our sins, suggesting that He does not deliver us from our sin nature and does not really expect us to change. That is a lie that is contrary to the whole teaching of the New Testament. The sin nature must be cut out of our lives.

We may stumble at times during the fight with the old nature, and there is grace and forgiveness for those who are fighting, but the Word of God is clear that there is no grace for those who embrace the sin as a tolerable lifestyle and refuse to call it sin. We will address some of those, but as we quoted the text from Galatians previously, it is clear that those who **"practice"** such things will not inherit the kingdom of God. There is a difference between practicing something and fighting it, though we may still be stumbling at times. For those who are struggling, we have the encouragement of Proverbs 24:16, **"For a righteous man falls seven times, and rises again."** Even "a righteous man" can be trapped in something he falls to over and over. However, "a righteous man" does not stay down but keeps getting up and keeps fighting.

I was once praying for a friend that could not seem to get free of his addiction to alcohol. I was given the above verse and told that his falling over and over did not displease the Lord as much as it pleased Him that he was determined to get up again and keep fighting.

Another one of my friends has been battling homosexuality for many years, to which he has occasionally fallen but he has never quit fighting. Neither has he ever tried to rationalize it away, but each remains committed to the truth and integrity of the Scriptures. Before the Lord, he may be more righteous than those who may not have had to struggle with this and are self-righteous about it.

Overcoming either of these battles is probably a bigger battle than I have ever had to fight, and those who do will probably be much stronger than those who never have to battle such things. Those who must overcome such strongholds may be worthy of double honor. However, we are told that those who give up or try to rationalize away the clear teaching of Scripture will have a greater condemnation. To even cause one of His little ones to stumble is so bad that He said it would be better for such a one to not even have been born (see Luke 17:2). We do not even want to contemplate what will happen on that great judgment day to those who promote a teaching that leaves many of His people in the grip of sin.

The only way one can justify such a theology of perpetual grace while practicing sin is to distort the Scriptures, which we are also told clearly will result in condemnation. The first fall of man was caused by the devil persuading Eve to question what God had clearly said and then changing it. This is the beginning of almost every fall since, and as the Scriptures clearly teach, those who do this will pay a terrible price. The wages of sin is death. The wages of causing others to stumble is obviously even worse.

At the end of Romans 7, the great apostle confesses that he himself was trapped in a cycle of sin where the things he did not want to do, he did, and the things he wanted to do, he could not. Everyone who has been a Christian for more than a few days has probably experienced this. A war is going on between our flesh and spirit, and the flesh is likely to win a few battles. The Lord does not condemn us for this but forgives our sins when we confess them.

He does not forgive excuses but instead sin that is confessed as sin. There is abundant grace for those who keep fighting and do not rationalize the sin. As we continue to fight, the Spirit will get stronger and the flesh weaker. Even so, the Lord is not trying to change us as much as kill us—our "old man" that is. We are putting to death the "body of death" so that we can be life to Him. There is also ultimately deliverance, as Paul goes on to explain:

> **There is therefore now no condemnation for those who are in Christ Jesus.**

> **For the law of the Spirit of life in Christ Jesus has set you free from the law of sin and of death.**

> **For what the Law could not do, weak as it was through the flesh, God *did*: sending His own Son in the likeness of sinful flesh and *as an offering* for sin, He condemned sin in the flesh,**

> **in order that the requirement of the Law might be fulfilled in us, who do not walk according to the flesh, but according to the Spirit (Romans 8:1-4).**

Every reference in the Old Testament to **"those uncircumcised"** is referring to the Philistines. The conflict and battles that Israel had with the Philistines continued through most of their history. Whenever the nation of Israel would fall away from their devotion to the Lord, they would be enslaved by the Philistines. Then the Philistines would come at their whim and plunder Israel, stealing their food, their wealth, and especially their weapons. Whenever the flesh, the carnal nature, gets the upper hand on us we will be enslaved to it, and it will then plunder our life and resources. Letting our flesh rule us will lead to slavery and poverty. The way that we defeat this deadly enemy is mostly to starve it, not setting our minds on the things of the flesh, and at the same time feeding our Spirit, as we read in Romans 8:5-17:

> For those who are according to the flesh set their minds on the things of the flesh, but those who are according to the Spirit, the things of the Spirit.
>
> For the mind set on the flesh is death, but the mind set on the Spirit is life and peace,
>
> because the mind set on the flesh is hostile toward God; for it does not subject itself to the law of God, for it is not even able *to do so*;
>
> and those who are in the flesh cannot please God.
>
> However, you are not in the flesh but in the Spirit, if indeed the Spirit of God dwells in you. But if anyone does not have the Spirit of Christ, he does not belong to Him.
>
> And if Christ is in you, though the body is dead because of sin, yet the spirit is alive because of righteousness.
>
> But if the Spirit of Him who raised Jesus from the dead dwells in you, He who raised Christ Jesus from the dead will also give life to your mortal bodies through His Spirit who indwells you.

So then, brethren, we are under obligation, not to the flesh, to live according to the flesh—

for if you are living according to the flesh, you must die; but if by the Spirit you are putting to death the deeds of the body, you will live.

For all who are being led by the Spirit of God, these are sons of God.

For you have not received a spirit of slavery leading to fear again, but you have received a spirit of adoption as sons by which we cry out, "Abba! Father!"

The Spirit Himself bears witness with our spirit that we are children of God,

and if children, heirs also, heirs of God and fellow heirs with Christ, if indeed we suffer with *Him* in order that we may also be glorified with *Him*.

This battle with the flesh can be won, and must be won. Like everything else, it is not meant to be easy. The Lord is seeking a people who care enough about Him, His people, and His purposes to fight for them and not give up until they have the victory. He is seeking a people who love what He loves and hate what He hates. He loves people, and He hates sin. Sin brought all of the death and suffering into this world and what He endured on the cross. He came to save us from sin, to give us life, and deliver us from death, because if we keep serving the carnal nature, we will die. If we keep seeking Him, and that which is above, we will live forever.

This is the deliverance from the death that is within, so that we might have life and be vessels of life. He came that He might give life. Death is the ultimate enemy of His purpose, and it must be defeated in our own hearts before we can go on into our inheritance.

The Worse Place It Could Happen

Gilgal was in the plain in front of Jericho. When Israel was enduring this circumcision, they were humiliated and made weak right within sight of their enemies. Why didn't the Lord have them do this before Israel crossed the Jordan? Have you ever wondered why so many of your battles with the flesh, especially such things as anger, strife, impatience, and so on, seem to always happen in front of the heathen? It especially seems to happen in front of those we are seeking to see come to the Lord. Why does the Lord let this happen and ruin our "witness?"

First, our being perfect is not the witness that leads others to salvation. What leads someone to salvation is for the Holy Spirit to convict them of sin, and to point them to Jesus and His cross which is the only remedy for sin. The only perfect witness is Jesus. That is why the apostolic message was to preach Jesus, not the church, not how good we are becoming, but Jesus. No one is ever really going to come to Jesus because they want to be like us. We should want to do good and walk by the Spirit because we want to live by the Spirit and please the Lord, not to have others look at us.

The point is that Jericho was able to see the Israelites as they really were—weak, humiliated, and needing to have their flesh cut away. Israel also knew that their enemies had seen them in their true condition. It is not about us but about the God we serve. If we would humble ourselves, the Lord would not have to do it. Let us just embrace humility now, not even expecting anyone to come to Christ because of how spiritual we are, but let us keep pointing to the One who is perfect, and they can examine Him all they want and never find a single flaw. Part of the work of this circumcision is to get rid of that pride—the attention we have on ourselves and want others to have on us.

The Great Deliverance

Remember, everything that literally happened with Israel is intended to be an outline for the spiritual conquest of our Promised Land. We are not seeking to drive the nations out like the Israelites did, but rather to give them life, leading them to salvation and liberty. In the next verses, we see how great this salvation we are pursuing for this world is:

> **For I consider that the sufferings of this present time are not worthy to be compared with the glory that is to be revealed to us.**
>
> **For the anxious longing of the creation waits eagerly for the revealing of the sons of God.**
>
> **For the creation was subjected to futility, not of its own will, but because of Him who subjected it, in hope**

that the creation itself also will be set free from its slavery to corruption into the freedom of the glory of the children of God.

For we know that the whole creation groans and suffers the pains of childbirth together until now (Romans 8:18-22).

This is basically saying that the whole creation that was under man, and has been subjected to the terrible consequences of the fall of man, is desperately waiting for man to be recovered and bring order back to this creation. The witness is not about us, but about Him. He is going to rule the world with His body, the church, and when she is ready He will take His authority over this world and restore it again to its original intention. The sooner "the bride makes herself ready," the sooner this can be accomplished.

Does this mean that we could actually speed up the coming of the Lord? In II Peter 3:12, he wrote that we should be **"looking for and hastening the coming of the day of God."** This does seem to indicate that we can actually speed up the coming of the day of the Lord. This is not just about us. He loves us personally and individually, and we do have an inheritance of unfathomable value in Him. When we have truly matured in Him, it will not be just about us or what we get, but about Him and seeing Him receive the reward of His sacrifice—the world that He loves recovered.

THE PASSOVER

The next thing the Israelites did before they were ready to attack the first stronghold and begin taking possession of their Promised Land was to celebrate the Passover. Of course, after the circumcision they needed to have a celebration! However, this was not just any celebration, but the greatest of all celebrations for Israel, and the one feast that the Israelites were commanded to celebrate every year for all generations.

It was the Passover that set them free from Egypt, and nothing else would have been possible without this. It is also crucial for this most basic of truths in their history to be perpetually remembered by such a celebration because, as stated, the most successful people in any field will always be those who do the basics best. This kept the Israelites moored to the most basic truths of the faith. The Passover also contains the most basic Christian truths, and is therefore crucial for us to review before we can go forward in the conquest of our Promised Land. As long as the Israelites were celebrating this feast, it kept them moored to the things that could give them victory over their enemies and success in all that they were called to do. It does the same for us as well. We will take this opportunity to review these basics again.

As stated in I Corinthians 5:7, "**Christ our Passover also has been sacrificed.**" Everything in the Passover speaks of Christ and what He accomplished for us on the cross. Just as it was the Passover sacrifice that delivered the Israelites from the power of Pharaoh so that her people would never again serve Egypt, it is the cross, of which the Passover was a prophetic type, that delivers us from the power of Satan and slavery to the corruption of the world. As the Passover did in type, the cross brings judgment upon the evils of the world and delivers all who will embrace it from the bondage.

A New Beginning

It was no accident that the first command that the Lord gave to the Israelites concerning the Passover was to change their calendar so that the date they partook of the first Passover would be the beginning of their year:

> **Now the LORD said to Moses and Aaron in the land of Egypt,**
>
> **"This month shall be the beginning of months for you; it is to be the first month of the year to you"** (Exodus 12:1-2).

140

Because of Passover, Israel's calendar was rotated so that the month of the Passover would be their first month, which was a prophecy of when we partake of the true Passover Lamb, Christ, that there will be a new beginning, and all things become new.

Therefore if any man be in Christ, he is a new creature: old things are passed away; behold, all things are become new (II Corinthians 5:17 KJV).

When Jesus becomes our Passover, we are born again into a new world. To the Israelites it was a physical change; to us it is a spiritual change. The external conditions and surroundings may remain the same, but we do not. If the externals suddenly appear different, it is because our eyes are new! When a person is born again, he begins to see the kingdom of God (see John 3:3). This is a far more glorious deliverance. Moses led Israel out of Egypt in one day, but "Egypt" (the ways of the world) still remained in Israel. Through Christ **"the world has been crucified to me, and I to the world" (see Galatians 6:14).** Jesus takes Egypt out of the heart and replaces it with a new country—the kingdom of God. Then, as we begin to see the kingdom of God, our perspective is changed. The more clearly we see Him sitting on His throne, the less we notice the problems and cares of the world.

To walk with God, we must walk in truth. As our vision of His kingdom is clarified, the things of earth do grow dim, and we begin to see a new reality. The things that are invisible to the natural man become more real to us than things that are seen. To those who do not see in the Spirit, this sounds absurd. The Apostle Paul explained:

> But a natural man does not accept the things of the Spirit of God; for they are foolishness to him, and he cannot understand them, because they are spiritually appraised.
>
> But he who is spiritual appraises all things [accurately], yet he himself is appraised by no man (I Corinthians 2:14-15).

Paul also wrote in Ephesians 1:18-23, the most basic principle of spiritual vision:

> I pray that the eyes of your heart may be enlightened, so that you may know what is the hope of His calling, what are the riches of the glory of His inheritance in the saints,
>
> and what is the surpassing greatness of His power toward us who believe. These are in accordance with the working of the strength of His might
>
> which He brought about in Christ, when He raised Him from the dead, and seated Him at His right hand in the heavenly places,
>
> far above all rule and authority and power and dominion, and every name that is named, not only in this age, but also in the one to come.
>
> And He put all things in subjection under His feet, and gave Him as head over all things to the church,

which is His body, the fullness of Him who fills all in all.

This is the essence of spiritual vision and seeing the kingdom of God—seeing Jesus, who He is and where He sits. *All* dominion has been given to Him, and nothing can happen that He does not allow. When the eyes of our hearts are opened to see this, it is difficult to give much credence to the cares of the world.

Elisha was a prophet who had this spiritual vision. When confronted by an entire army, he sat peacefully on the side of a hill, much to his servant's dismay. When Elisha prayed for the servant's eyes to be opened, the servant was then able to understand the reason for Elisha's confidence—the angels standing for them outnumbered the enemy (see II Kings 6:8-23). Likewise, in any circumstance, those with a heavenly perspective know that those who are with us greatly outnumber those who are against us.

Walking in the Spirit

One of the ancient saints wrote of the new creation man, which we are to be after we partake of the Passover of Christ: "We are not just human beings who have occasional spiritual experiences, but we are spiritual beings who have occasional human experiences." To walk in the Spirit is to see with His eyes, hear with His ears, and understand with His heart. As we do this, the earth, with all of its problems and its glories, begins to appear as small as it really is. After we have beheld the glory and authority of Jesus, kings and presidents are no more impressive than the destitute. Once we have seen the Lord, all earthly pomp and position appear ludicrous, and even the worst international crisis is hardly cause for concern. The King is on His throne, and He will never lose control.

When Isaiah saw the Lord sitting on His throne, there were seraphim with Him who called out to one another, **"Holy, Holy, Holy, is the LORD of hosts,** *the whole earth is full of His glory*" **(see Isaiah 6:3)**. With all of the wars, conflicts, disasters, diseases, famines, and confusion among nations, how can the seraphim say that **"the whole earth is full of His glory"**? They are able to say it because they dwell in the presence of the Lord. Those who dwell in His presence will likewise see the whole earth as being full of His glory. The Lord will prevail, and His truth will ultimately prevail over all lies. We can see the reality of what is taking place on earth, but we also see the greater reality of God's plan and power. We are citizens of the new creation, not the old, and we must see from the perspective of the new.

Now we might ask why we have this continual battle with our old nature if we are new creatures. We would not have this battle if we kept our eyes on Jesus. It is when we, like Peter, take our eyes off of Him and focus on the tossing waves of the world and the flesh that we begin to sink again into the old ways and perspectives. This is not easy, especially as the storms grow all around us, but it is essential, especially for the coming times.

Without Christ, there is no good thing in us. Without Christ, there is no true hope for the world. No matter how many times we look at ourselves or at the circumstances, we will find the same thing—evil. But in Christ we no longer have to live by our sinful nature. He has given us His Life, His Spirit! When He said, **"It is finished" (see John 19:30),** He meant it. He is the finished work of God; He is the finished work the Father seeks to accomplish in us.

Maturity is not accomplished by striving to reach a certain level of spirituality—maturity is simply abiding in Him who is the finished work of God. Jesus *is* our wisdom, righteousness, sanctification, and redemption (see I Corinthians1:30). Jesus is everything we are called to be; we can only fulfill our calling by abiding in Him.

We will never become the new creation simply by setting spiritual goals or even attaining them. We can only attain true spirituality by abiding in the One who *is* the work of God. Jesus is the Alpha and Omega, the Beginning and the End of all things. Jesus is called **"the first-born of all creation" (see Colossians 1:15).** Jesus is the whole Purpose of God. Everything that the Father loved and esteemed, He brought forth in His Son. Everything was created *by* Him and *for* Him, and *in* Him all things hold together (see Colossians 1:16-17). The whole creation was *for* the Son. All things are to be summed up in Him (see Ephesians 1:10). We accomplish the whole purpose of God in our lives when we have our whole being summed up in Him by simply abiding.

> See to it that no one takes you captive through philosophy and empty deception, according to the tradition of men, according to the elementary principles of the world, rather than according to Christ.
>
> For in Him all the fulness of Deity dwells in bodily form,
>
> and in Him you have been made complete (see Colossians 2:8-10).

If we do not stay focused on the ultimate purpose of God—that all things will be summed up in Christ—we will be continually distracted by the lesser purposes of God, or even worse, by the interests of the world.

The new birth is possibly the greatest demonstration of the love and grace of God. We have all sinned and are worthy of death. However, the Father so loved us that He sent His own Son to be a propitiation offering for our sins, allowing us to start over again. We exchange our body of death for eternal life as the Lord's own children. No genius of fantasy or fiction could have ever dreamed a more wonderful story. How could we who have partaken of such glory not **"do all things for the sake of the gospel?" (see I Corinthians 9:23)** Our ultimate goal should be to walk in truth that Paul wrote:

> *For the love of Christ controls us,* having concluded this, that one died for all, therefore all died;
>
> and He died for all, *that they who live should no longer live for themselves, but*

for Him who died and rose again on their behalf (II Corinthians 5:14-15).

Taking the Lamb Into the House

Speak to all the congregation of Israel, saying, "On the tenth of this month they are each one to take a lamb for themselves, according to their fathers' households, a lamb for each household.

"And you shall keep it until the fourteenth day of the same month" (see Exodus 12:3, 6).

The purpose of taking the lamb into the house five days before the sacrifice was to carefully examine it for flaws. This was a prophecy that Jesus, the true Passover Lamb, would enter Jerusalem five days before His crucifixion. He did this, perfectly fulfilling the prophecy. While He was entering the city, the ritual Passover lambs were themselves being taken into the houses all over Israel.

As these lambs were being examined for disqualifying flaws, the scribes, Pharisees, and Sadducees were challenging Jesus, trying to find a flaw in the Lamb of God. Despite their most intense challenges, they could find no flaw in Him. He was the acceptable sacrifice for God's Passover. The rulers finally resigned themselves to hiring false witnesses against Him.

In John 19:42, we note that Jesus was slain on the Jewish Day of Preparation. On this day, all the Passover lambs were slain to prepare for the feast. As Jesus was nailed to the cross, knives were being put to the throats of sacrificial lambs throughout Israel. The fulfillment of the type was taking place right in their midst, right on time.

Jesus alone is the Lamb who is without blemish. Our acceptance by the Father has already been determined at the cross and is therefore not based on how well we have done or are doing now. Our ability to come boldly before the throne of grace must never be measured by how good or bad we have been, but by the blood of Jesus. Coming on any other basis is an affront to the sacrifice He made for us on the cross. The cross alone has gained our approval from God.

True ministry is not done in order to gain God's approval, but rather it comes from a position of *having* His approval. We have His approval because of the cross of Jesus, never because of our own works. We labor because we love Him, and we long to see Him receive the reward of His sacrifice. There is a vast difference between trying to please God because we love Him and trying to please Him in order to gain His acceptance. The former is worship; the latter is still the self-seeking pursuit of self-righteousness that is the root of an evil religious spirit.

He Was Crucified By Us

> *The whole assembly* of the congregation of Israel is to kill it [the lamb] at twilight (see Exodus 12:6).

And *all the people* answered and said, "His blood be on us and on our children" (Matthew 27:25).

As was prophesied by the type, it was the whole congregation of Israel that delivered Jesus to be crucified. Yet it was not just Israel that crucified Him; it was the carnal nature that is within us all. Had the Lord chosen to send His Son to any other nation, there would have been the same result. Even Plato perceived that a truly righteous man would be despised by all men and would eventually be impaled, which was the Greek equivalent of crucifixion.

In Matthew 25:45, the Lord Jesus stated, **"Truly I say to you, to the extent that you did not do it to one of the least of these, you did not do it to Me."** We must stop crucifying the Lord again in each other. Instead, we need to start esteeming the Lord and His workmanship in each one, giving the value to one another which He gave. Few things will work to the edification of the whole body of Christ so much as our starting to know each other after the Spirit instead of after the flesh. Let us pray to only see each other with His eyes, hear with His ears, and understand with His heart.

Because the Word is also clear that we will reap what we sow (see Galatians 6:7), if we want to receive grace, we need to sow it every chance we get. If we want to receive mercy, we need to extend it every chance we get. We should be looking for every opportunity to forgive people, show them mercy, and give them grace.

The Life Is In the Blood

> **Moreover, they shall take some of the blood and put it on the two doorposts and on the lintel of the houses in which they eat it (Exodus 12:7).**

The angel of death could not touch the houses that had the lamb's blood applied to them. Without the blood, they would have been doomed to the same judgment that came upon Egypt. It is by the application of the blood of Jesus to our lives that we are freed from God's judgment against the world and its sin, the wages of that sin being death. Nothing more, or less, will save us.

It would not have done Israel any good to have sacrificed the Passover lamb *unless they also applied its blood to their houses.* Likewise, it will not benefit us to realize that a propitiation for our sins was needed or even to know that Jesus made that propitiation—*unless His blood is applied to our lives.* To just know facts without applying them accomplishes nothing. Even the demons know and believe the doctrine of salvation. It is not knowing in our minds, but believing in our hearts, which brings salvation (see Romans 10:9-10).

Communion

> **And they shall eat the flesh that same night, roasted with fire, and they shall eat it with unleavened bread and bitter herbs (Exodus 12:8).**

Jesus therefore said to them, "Truly, truly, I say to you, unless you eat the flesh of the Son of Man and drink His blood, you have no life in yourselves" (John 6:53).

"We are what we eat" is a common axiom, but it is just as true in relation to our spiritual food. If we are partaking of the Lord Jesus, the Tree of Life, we will become that Life. Jesus did not say "he who has eaten My flesh" but "he who *eats*," or he who continues to eat. This speaks of our need to continually partake of Him and abide in Him. He is the true Manna from heaven (see John 6:58). Just as the Israelites had to gather fresh manna each day because it would spoil if stored, we, too, must seek Him afresh each day. We cannot be sustained on day-old revelation. We cannot set aside one day a week to be spiritual and expect to abide in Him the rest of the week. He must be new to us every morning.

When the Lord referred to the eating of His flesh and drinking of His blood, of course He was not talking of His physical flesh and blood, but rather what they symbolically represented—His life and His body, the church (we are bone of His bone and flesh of His flesh). Perplexed by what He said, most of those who heard this departed from Him (see John 6:66). This remains today the main place where believers depart from Him, and they seek to replace the real communion with a ritual.

To partake of the ritual is not equivalent to partaking of Him. The ritual of communion was given as a reminder, not a substitute. When this ritual usurps the reality, the very life of the Lord is removed from the church. The Apostle Paul explained the meaning of this rite to the Corinthians:

> **The cup of blessing which we bless, is it not the communion of the blood of Christ? The bread which we break, is it not the communion of the body of Christ? (I Corinthians 10:16 KJV)**

Communion was originally two words which were merged to form one—*COMMON* and *UNION*. This translates from the Greek *KOINONIA*, which is defined as "the using of a thing in common." We are not brought together by the bread and wine, but by what they symbolically represent—the body and blood of Jesus. The ceremony we call communion is not an *actual* communion; it is a symbolic testimony that those partaking of it have a *common-union* in Christ. As Paul warned the Corinthians:

> **For I received from the Lord that which I also delivered to you, that the Lord Jesus in the night in which He was betrayed took bread;**
>
> **and when He had given thanks, He broke it, and said, "This is My body, which is for you; do this in REMEMBRANCE of Me."**
>
> **In the same way He took the cup also, after supper, saying, "This cup is the new covenant in My blood; do this, as often as you drink it, in REMEMBRANCE of Me."**

For as often as you eat this bread and drink the cup, you proclaim the Lord's death until He comes.

Therefore whoever eats the bread or drinks the cup of the Lord in an unworthy manner, shall be guilty of the body and the blood of the Lord.

But let a man examine himself, and so let him eat of the bread and drink of the cup.

For he who eats and drinks, eats and drinks judgment to himself, if he does not judge the body rightly.

For this reason many among you are weak and sick, and a number sleep (I Corinthians 11:23-30).

If we do not discern the body of Christ rightly, we are pronouncing judgment upon ourselves when we partake of the bread and wine. That is, if we participate in the ritual assuming it fulfills our obligation to commune with Christ, we have deceived ourselves; we remain deprived of true Life.

The substitution of rituals for realities has repeatedly deprived people of redemption and salvation. **"For this reason many among you are weak and sick, and a number sleep."** If a member of our physical body was cut off from the rest of the body, it would become weak and die very fast. The same happens when we cut ourselves off from our spiritual body, the church.

The Apostle John declared, **"but if we walk in the light as He Himself is in the light, we have fellowship**

[Greek *koinonia*: communion] **with one another, and the blood of Jesus His Son cleanses us from all sin"** (I John 1:7). The Lord said the life is **"in the blood" (see Leviticus 17:11).** If we "commune" with Him, we are joined in one body under the Head so His life's blood can flow through us.

Being properly joined to the body of Christ is not an option if true life is going to flow through us. Just as I shared earlier, when I was shown that the bird flu plague was certainly coming, I was also shown that the only place of safety from it was to be in His house, the church. It is the only safe place at all on this earth. If we are rightly connected to the Head, Jesus, we will also be rightly connected to His body, which means we will be in our right place in His body. It was a hard saying then, which caused many of His disciples to depart from Him, and it is still a hard saying today, which continues to cause many to depart from Him.

I have heard many say that they love the Lord, but they just don't like His people. However, we are told in I John 4:20-21 that this cannot be true, **"If someone says, 'I love God,' and hates his brother, he is a liar; for the one who does not love his brother whom he has seen, cannot love God whom he has not seen. And this commandment we have from Him, that the one who loves God should love his brother also."**

If we love Him, we will also love His people, and if we love them, we will find our place in His body, the church, in order to serve Him and His family—anything less than this is deception. This deception is still the main reason for the weakness, sickness, and premature death among Christians.

We Must Eat the Whole Thing

Do not eat any of it raw or boiled at all with water, but rather roasted with fire, both its head and its legs along with its entrails.

And you shall not leave any of it over until morning (see Exodus 12:9-10).

Some have become very particular about the gospel, as if it were up to them to choose the aspects of redemption they need. If we are to partake of the Lord's Passover, we must accept every part. He did not give us the option to take what we want. As He stated in the parable, when we find the pearl of great price, we must buy the whole field in which it was found (see Matthew 13:46).

When the Lord commissioned His followers to go and make disciples of all nations, He specifically included **"teaching them to observe ALL that I commanded you" (see Matthew 28:20).** When we come with pre-conditions of which of His commandments we will accept, we void the very power of the gospel. Often it is that which represents the greatest threat to us that we need the most.

The specific matter that intimidates us is not the important issue; to pick and choose what *we* want is a rejection of His lordship. He cannot be received as our Savior unless He also comes as our Lord. It is the acceptance of His full lordship that delivers us from the self-centeredness that kills us. Those who claim to have received Him as Savior but continue living according to their own will are deceived. True salvation is the deliverance from self-will and our self-life in exchange for His life. If He is not the Lord *of* all, He is not the Lord *at* all.

When we compromise the gospel to make it acceptable or for any other reason, we strip it of the power to save. Deliverance from the power of evil is not accomplished by merely "turning over a new leaf" and making a few changes in our lives. True deliverance saves us from the "I WILL" so firmly rooted in our fallen nature.

The Passover sacrifice of Jesus did not just "paint over" us with His blood; it cleansed us and destroyed the angel of death, the body of sin, and our self-will. Any gospel that preaches salvation without complete surrender is without salvation as well. It is an enemy of the true gospel. A compromised gospel only immunizes us to the truth or gives us just enough of it to make us resistant to the whole. As the Lord made clear: **"For whoever wishes to save his life shall lose it; but whoever loses his life for My sake shall find it"** (Matthew 16:25).

If we want His life, we must be willing to share His death. When the Lord called a man, he had to leave everything: **"So therefore, no one of you can be My disciple who does not give up all his own possessions"** (Luke 14:33). Whether He requires this of

156

us literally or just in our hearts, it must be real and total. We must all learn the lessons of Job who had to lose everything except the Lord before he knew that the Lord was all he needed. A man who stands in need of nothing but Jesus will not be bound by anything or anyone but Him.

The church today is fragmented into different camps that gather around certain truths of the gospel. We have assumed the freedom to choose for ourselves which parts of the body of Christ we will accept and which parts we will reject. It is a natural tendency to gravitate toward that which is most comfortable, those who agree with us, but this is also the path to perpetual spiritual immaturity. The result has been a debilitating imbalance in most congregations. Those with an evangelistic burden are found in one group; those with a pastoral burden in another; the prophets in still another. One congregation is all "feet," another "hands," and another "eyes." These bodies are grotesque substitutes for the perfect body that Christ is determined to have.

Each member must be properly joined to the others if the body is to function correctly. Having a perfect heart would be of no benefit without the lungs, kidneys, liver, etc. We presently have all hearts in one place claiming to be the body, all livers in another, and so forth. There must be interchange, interrelationship, and the proper joining of the different parts of the body before there can be an effective functioning of the same.

Pastors have a God-given cautious nature that is intended to be protective of God's people. Prophets are visionary by nature, but they are also often reckless. Without the balance and influence of the prophetic ministry, pastors will tend to stagnate and become set in their ways. Without the influence of pastors, prophets will drift into extremes, having visions which no one knows how to practically fulfill.

Teachers usually will be very pragmatic in nature, which is essential for clear impartation of the Word. But without prodding from the other ministries, they tend to reduce life in Christ to principles and formulas that are learned by rote. Evangelists, given to focus on the needs of the lost, often forget to raise and mature them. Yet without evangelists, the church will quickly forget the unsaved. Because apostles are called to be evangelists, prophets, pastors, and teachers, they usually have a more balanced nature and are given for the purpose of keeping the church on the right path.

The unity of the Spirit is not a unity of conformity; it is a unity of diversity. In fact, the church was intended to be the first true university, or unity-in-diversity. For this reason, the Lord gave diverse ministries—apostles, prophets, evangelists, pastors, and teachers—to equip the saints (see Ephesians 4:11-12). We must receive *all* the ministries. To partake of the Lord's body, we must "eat the whole thing."

We are exhorted to **"grow up in *all* aspects into Him, who is the head" (see Ephesians 4:15).** The apostles were directed to **"speak to the people in the temple the whole message of this Life" (see Acts 5:20).**

The psalmist discerned that **"the SUM of Thy word is truth" (see Psalm 119:160).** We can be distracted from the Truth by individual truths. We can be distracted from the River of Life by the individual tributaries which feed it.

Individual aspects of God's Word may be interpreted falsely apart from the whole Word. The Lord emphasized the fact that the Scriptures have eternal life only if they testify of Him (see John 5:39-40). Overbalance in one area is indicative of partial, incomplete comprehension of the whole. As Paul explained to the Hebrews, **"God, after He spoke long ago to the fathers in the prophets in many portions and in many ways, in these last days has spoken to us in His Son" (see Hebrews 1:1-2).** The Father is no longer giving us fragments. He has given us the whole Loaf.

We may have such a vision of the united and perfected body of Christ that we are sure the church will draw all men to itself. However, the church is not to draw men to itself, but rather is commissioned to equip those whom the Lord has drawn. It is only when Jesus is lifted up that all men will be drawn together, and they will be drawn to HIM! King David perceived this and wrote the "Psalm of Unity": **"Behold, how good and how pleasant it is for brothers to dwell together in unity! It is like the precious oil UPON THE HEAD** [Jesus]**, coming down upon the beard . . . coming down upon the edge of his robes"** (Psalm 133:1-2).

If we anoint the Head with our worship and devotion, the oil will run down and cover the whole body (of Christ). One day there will be a church perfected in unity, but it is likely that she will not even be aware of how glorious she is. Her attention will be on Jesus, not herself.

The Spirit Moves

Now you shall eat it in this manner: with your loins girded, your sandals on your feet, and your staff in your hand; and you shall eat it in haste (see Exodus 12:11).

Included in the Passover was the Feast of Unleavened Bread (see Exodus 12:14-20). For seven days, beginning with the first day of the Passover, Israel could not eat any leavened bread. This was meant to remind the Israelites of their flight from Egypt, when they left in such haste that their bread did not have time to become leavened:

And they baked the dough which they had brought out of Egypt into cakes of unleavened bread. For it had not become leavened, since they were driven out of Egypt and could not delay (see Exodus 12:39).

Because of its permeating characteristics, leaven (yeast) is often used as a symbol of sin in Scripture:

Do you not know that a little leaven leavens the whole lump of dough?

Clean out the old leaven, that you may be a new lump, just as you are in fact unleavened. For Christ our Passover also has been sacrificed.

**Let us therefore celebrate the feast, not
with old leaven, nor with the leaven of malice
and wickedness, but with the unleavened
bread of sincerity and truth (see I Corinthians 5:6-8).**

Leaven is also symbolic of doctrine that is legalistic
in nature. The Lord warned His disciples to **"beware
of the leaven of the Pharisees and Sadducees" (see Matthew 16:6).** Israel's bread did not have time to become
leavened because Egypt was left in such haste. In the
same way, if we will keep moving with the Spirit, our
"bread" will not have time to become leavened with
sin, wickedness, or legalism. It is when we stop moving
and growing that our "bread" becomes infected.

We addressed how the Passover lamb was taken
into the houses of Israel to be thoroughly examined
for five days before the sacrifice, and how this may
reflect the need to thoroughly examine Christ before
making a commitment. Yet we see here that once the
commitment is made, we must then move in haste to
flee the land of Egypt.

There is something about continual movement in
the Lord that is required for spiritual health. One of
the metaphors for truth is water, and water must keep
flowing to stay pure. Of course, there are also times
where we will be required to wait on the Lord and
learn to be still in His presence. Even then, we should
be seeking Him and growing in our understanding
of His ways. Generally, the life in the Spirit is not a
static life but one of dynamic movement and constant

growth. When we stop, that is when we tend to get into trouble with either sin or legalism.

No Strangers May Eat of It

> **This is the ordinance of the Passover: no foreigner** [stranger] **is to eat of it (see Exodus 12:43).**

As the church grows in the grace and knowledge of our Lord, we should become more tolerant in certain ways, but this does not mean we will be all-inclusive. Inclusion in the true church requires a true commitment to Christ as our Savior and Lord and certain basic standards of behavior and integrity.

Jesus is the Door. A door has two functions—to let people in and to keep them out. When we allow those to join the church who have not come through the Door, we place both the congregation and the unconverted in jeopardy. This is not to say that unsaved people should be excluded from our services, but they should not be included as members of the body of Christ until they have been joined to the Head.

The first thing which God said was **"not good"** (see **Genesis 2:18**) was for man to be alone. He made us social creatures and therefore we all crave strong social ties. The true church is the most dynamic social entity the world has ever known. We must be careful that people are not drawn to our assemblies instead of to the Lord. It is common for people to say the right things, change their outward behavior, and even sincerely believe the doctrine of Christ in their minds without knowing Jesus in their hearts. It is possible to be quite "spiritual" and yet not know Him, as the Lord Himself warned:

> "Many will say to Me on that day, 'Lord, Lord, did we not prophesy in Your name, and in Your name cast out demons, and in Your name perform many miracles?'
>
> "And then I will declare to them, 'I never knew you; depart from Me, you who practice lawlessness'" (Matthew 7:22-23).
>
> "As the branch cannot bear fruit of itself, unless it abides in the vine, so neither can you, unless you abide in Me" (see John 15:4).

To be joined to the church through Christ is life and power. Seeking union with Christ through the church is vain. It is truth that one cannot be joined to Christ without being joined to His body, but we have often made it easy for one to be attached to the body without being joined to the Head. This will ultimately cause many problems, not to mention possibly putting the very salvation of some in jeopardy by allowing them to think they are a part of Christ, when they have not truly given their life to Him or been born again.

The Victory

> Now the sons of Israel had done according to the word of Moses, for they had requested from the Egyptians articles of silver and articles of gold, and clothing;

> **and the LORD had given the people favor in the sight of the Egyptians, so that they let them have their request. Thus they plundered the Egyptians (Exodus 12:35-36).**

After being slaves for four hundred years, Israel partook of the Passover and became wealthier than in their wildest imagination. When we partake of the true Passover, which is Christ, in Him we are given the right to become the sons of God—joint heirs of the world and all it contains. Even so, all of the world's riches are nothing compared to the spiritual riches that are in Christ. **"But just as it is written, 'Things which eye has not seen and ear has not heard, and which have not entered the heart of man, all that God has prepared for those who love Him'" (I Corinthians 2:9).** Truly, in Christ we have inherited more riches than we are capable of imagining.

Israel left Egypt weighed down with wealth, but they were not taken to the closest bazaar so they could spend it. God took them into the wilderness where they could not spend even a single shekel! There they were able to invest their riches toward something more valuable than anything the world could sell them—the tabernacle, a habitation for God so He might dwell among them.

Today, the body of Christ receives a great deal of teaching about the riches we have in Christ. This teaching is timely. For centuries, the church has been deprived of the inheritance she has in Christ. Unfortunately, much of this emphasis has been devoted more to the material than the eternal. This is the delusion of slaves who one day dramatically find themselves kings. However, it is encouraging that many are beginning to reject the mentality that is overly devoted to the material and give themselves to the incomparable riches of Christ.

Blessed be the God and Father of our Lord Jesus Christ, who has blessed us with every spiritual blessing in the heavenly places in Christ (Ephesians 1:3).

When we perceive our *spiritual* blessings in Christ, *material* blessings lose their appeal. If we were to discover a vein of gold that could provide the entire world's needs forever, would we continue panning for mere nuggets? We have that Vein in the person of Jesus. Why do we give so much attention to the temporal, material things when we can be with God? It can only be because we have not truly seen Him as He is; we have merely discovered a few things about Him.

A cave will have more glory if the Lord is in it than the greatest palace. To live in a cave or palace will make little difference if we abide in Him. Some think it is more spiritual to be abased materially and others think it is more spiritual to abound, but neither is true. We may be in error if we are trying to live an abased life that God has not called us to or vice versa. The issue is being in the will of the Lord and keeping a steadfast devotion to Him whether we are abounding or being abased.

165

Though extremes can be in every teaching, and certainly some extremes are in the "prosperity teachings," there is also much in this teaching that the body of Christ needs in order to fulfill our calling. Even so, some elements to this teaching can distract us from our calling. The truly spiritual person is one because his heart is so captured by the things of the Spirit that he simply has little time or interest for the things of the world. Once we have beheld the spiritual riches that are found in Christ, going back to worldly interests could be compared to a billionaire sweeping streets for minimum wage. Those who still have an over-devotion for worldly pleasures simply have not received the love of the Father (see I John 2:15).

Even so, true spirituality is not just distaste for the world and its interests; it is a consuming love for the things of the Spirit and the interests of our God. This can only come when the eyes of our hearts have been opened so that the things of the Spirit are more real to us than the things that are seen with the eyes of our minds. If we have this mindset, we may be trusted with much more in this world because it will not capture our hearts and become an idol where we start to put our affections and trust in more than God. If we have truly given our lives to Him, then we are all stewards for His sake.

The Waving of the Sheaf

As a fitting last touch to this remarkable Feast of the Passover, the Lord instituted what is called "The

Waving of the Sheaf of the Firstfruits" (see Leviticus 23:9-15). This feast was celebrated in early spring as the first shoots of the coming harvest were just sprouting. On the morning after the Passover Sabbath, a sheaf of this first evidence of the coming harvest was brought to the priest and he waved it before the Lord. As this ritual was being performed after the Passover of our Lord's crucifixion, Jesus was bursting forth from His tomb! Jesus was the Sheaf of the firstfruits of the resurrection, who at that very time was being waved before the Father as evidence of the coming great harvest, perfectly fulfilling the type.

An interesting fact is that more Scripture is devoted to Abraham choosing a burial place for his family than to such important subjects as being born again or church order. Isaac and Jacob insisted on being buried there, and Joseph made the sons of Israel swear to carry his bones up from Egypt to bury him there. It is a great enigma as to why the patriarchs gave so much importance to where they were to be buried, until we read Matthew 27:50-53:

> And Jesus cried out again with a loud voice, and yielded up His spirit.
>
> And behold, the veil of the temple was torn in two from top to bottom, and the earth shook; and the rocks were split,
>
> and the tombs were opened; and many bodies of the saints who had fallen asleep were raised;

and coming out of the tombs *after His resurrection* **they entered the holy city and appeared to many.**

The burial ground which Abraham had chosen for his family was in Hebron, just outside of Jerusalem. As the Lord Himself confirmed, Abraham was a prophet who had foreseen His resurrection: **"Your father Abraham rejoiced to see My day, and he saw it and was glad" (John 8:56).** Abraham and those of his family who had vision made a provision to be a part of the first resurrection.

The patriarchs were not just concerned about where they were buried, but where they would be raised. Those who have vision are also making provision by how they are buried as to how they will be raised. If we have been buried with Christ, we shall also be raised with Him (see Romans 6:5). Every Christian is called to be a martyr—every day! We make provision for our resurrection every day, by laying down our lives and being buried with Him. In this light, one of the greatest men of vision of all time gave the church what may be his most important exhortation:

For we are the true circumcision, who worship in the Spirit of God and glory in Christ Jesus and put no confidence in the flesh,

More than that, I count all things to be loss in view of the surpassing value of knowing Christ Jesus my Lord, for whom I have suffered the loss of all things, and count them but rubbish in order that I may gain Christ,

and may be found in Him, not having a righteousness of my own derived from the Law, but that which is through faith in Christ, the righteousness which comes from God on the basis of faith,

that I may know Him, and the power of His resurrection and the fellowship of His sufferings, being conformed to His death;

in order that I may attain to the resurrection from the dead.

Not that I have already obtained it, or have already become perfect, but I press on in order that I may lay hold of that for which also I was laid hold of by Christ Jesus.

Brethren, I do not regard myself as having laid hold of it yet; but one thing I do: forgetting what lies behind and reaching forward to what lies ahead,

I press on toward the goal for the prize of the upward call of God in Christ Jesus (**Philippians 3:3, 8-14**).

Paul's declaration, **"one thing I do,"** reflects the singleness of his mind on this issue. When our eyes, or vision, is likewise single, our whole body will be full of light. Only then will we know true resurrection life and power.

Conclusion

These are the most basic issues of the faith that we should regularly review. After celebrating this first

Passover in the Promised Land, Israel was ready to begin possessing it. We, too, can expect a fresh and deeper revelation to come of Jesus as our Passover as we are prepared to begin the battle for our inheritance.

When Israel celebrated their feasts, they did not just get together and eat, but they recounted the great events of their history, the ways that the Lord had led them, provided for them, and revealed His ways to them. The Lord did mandate more feasts than fasts, and He obviously loved for His people to celebrate and enjoy one another as they did this in His presence. In this way, they fortified their faith and the knowledge of His ways, while expressing their thanksgiving for His love and care for them. All of this is still crucial for us.

Immediately after Israel celebrated the Passover on the plains before Jericho, the next great event took place that was required before they could go any further— the Captain of the hosts of the Lord met them. In Part Two, we will begin our next study—coming to know the Lord as the Captain of His army and how His people will become the army they are called to be, and begin to face and bring down the biggest evil strongholds of our times, taking dominion over their inheritance in Christ. At this writing, the church may still look like a huge, mixed mob, but this will soon change, and the most powerful force for good the world has seen in nearly two thousand years will march again, and this time for its ultimate purpose.

BECOME A
MORNINGSTAR
PARTNER

MorningStar is equipping the body of
Christ through our schools, missions,
conferences, television shows, and
publications. We need partners who will
join with us to help raise up and send out
those who have the potential to be the most
high-impact ministries possibly in church
history. If you have a heart for impacting
your generation, then consider partnering
with us today.

CSCL

ZAO

Heritage

Conferences

In His Service,

MorningStar Partners

JOIN TODAY

◆ JOIN ONLINE AT
   WWW.MORNINGSTARMINISTRIES.ORG

◆ CALL 1-800-542-0278

MorningStar University
O N L I N E

JOIN THE
REVOLUTION

MorningStar University (MSU) Online
is a real time, webstreamed, and
interactive study program. MSU Online
provides timeless teaching and
strategic training, but it also includes
timely prophetic insight because it is
based in real time. MSU Online
provides you with a digital,
web-based seat in the
classroom of MorningStar
University.

For more information email:
MSUonline@MorningStarMinistries.org

NEW
E-Journal

One Full Year
ONLY
$10
Item # EMAG

The Morning Star
JOURNAL®

This is our flagship publication, and contributors include some of the most important teachers and prophetic voices in our times. Distributed in nearly 100 nations, this is fuel for vision for those determined to press beyond the present limits.

One Full Year
ONLY
$20
Item # MAG

THE KINGDOM

KINGDOM AUTHORITY

Journal

Foreign subscription
$30.00USD Item # FMAG

To order your subscription:

Call 1-800-542-0278, visit us online at www.MorningStarMinistries.org
or write to 375 Star Light Drive, Fort Mill, SC 29715.

• Shipping is included. • No other discounts apply to this service.
Prices may be subject to change without notice.

WEBSTREAMING

Be Here...
Even When You
Can't Be Here

streaming 300kbps

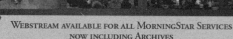

WEBSTREAM AVAILABLE FOR ALL MorningStar SERVICES
NOW INCLUDING ARCHIVES

LIVE WEBSTREAM	V.O.D. ONLY (VIDEO ON DEMAND)	LIVE WEBSTREAM WITH 30 DAY V.O.D.
$ 5 AUDIO PER MONTH	$ 8 AUDIO PER MONTH	$10 AUDIO PER MONTH
$10 VIDEO PER MONTH	$15 VIDEO PER MONTH	$20 VIDEO PER MONTH

INCLUDES **BREAKOUT** MEETINGS, SCHOOL OF THE SPIRIT,
SCHOOL OF THE WORD, AND SUNDAY MORNING SERVICES.

FOR MORE INFORMATION OR TO SUBSCRIBE:
CALL 1-800-542-0278

OR VISIT US ONLINE AT:
WWW.MORNINGSTARMINISTRIES.ORG

COMENIUS
School *for* Creative Leadership

CSCL is an innovative Christian K-12 school which seeks to raise up the next generation of leaders by equipping students to tap into their God-given gifts and talents.

FOR MORE INFORMATION:

Email: CSCL@MorningStarMinistries.org
Call: 803-547-3223

MorningStar PC Study Bible

We believe this is the most powerful, easy to use Bible and christian research program available, and it would be a value at several times this price. —Rick Joyner

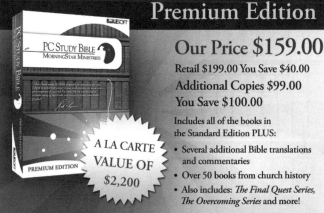

Premium Edition

Our Price $159.00

Retail $199.00 You Save $40.00

Additional Copies $99.00
You Save $100.00

Includes all of the books in
the Standard Edition PLUS:

- Several additional Bible translations
  and commentaries
- Over 50 books from church history
- Also includes: *The Final Quest Series,
  The Overcoming Series* and more!

A LA CARTE VALUE OF $2,200

Standard Edition

Our Price $79.00

Retail $99.00 You Save $20.00

Additional Copies $49.00
You Save $50.00

Includes:

- Multiple Bible Translations
- Complete Bible Commentary
- Bible History Collection
- Maps, Photos, & Much More
- PLUS: Nine of MorningStar's Books

A LA CARTE VALUE OF $860